the **well-dressed** salad

CONTEMPORARY, DELICIOUS AND SATISFYING RECIPES FOR SALADS

JENNIFER JOYCE

PHOTOGRAPHY BY SIAN IRVINE

whitecap

contents

introduction

My obsession with salads began in childhood. I grew up in rural Wisconsin in the north-central United States, surrounded by lush orchards and fertile farmland. My father, Leo, kept an enormous vegetable garden to help feed our family of eleven. Although I cursed the long hours of weeding and laborious end-of-summer bottling, I loved the earthy smell of the garden, its astounding variety, and eating juicy, ripe vegetables straight off the vine. My Italian mother, Louise, had to be an efficient household manager, of course, but she was more than that. She was also an artful cook. Delicious food was the one extravagance allowed. Since vegetables were plentiful, we had salads with every meal. Most were simple but intensely good: cucumbers, onions and tomatoes or roasted (bell) peppers dressed with red wine vinegar and olive oil. My favourite part of eating salad came at its pungent end. I would wipe the last vinegary remnants with bread and savour the final tart tastes. It's those mouth-watering memories that spur me to seek out ingredients as exceptional as the produce grown in my father's garden and transformed at my mother's table.

In the dozen years I've lived in London, England, my cooking has been influenced by many different cultures and synthesized into what I call modern ethnic food. Although the classes I teach each week might cover Vietnamese or Middle Eastern cooking, Californian cuisine or North African tastes, all my dishes have one thing in common – the pursuit of bold, fresh flavours. I am passionate about combining herbs, vinegars and unusual ethnic products to create extraordinary flavours. You won't, for instance, find many mayonnaise dressings here, because flavours should be enhanced, not smothered.

I decided to write this book after designing a class on salads and finding it difficult to pare down my salad choices. I love them all, from the great Thai varieties to the perfect Caesar. I also began to realize just how well salads work for the way we live now, reflecting our new awareness about healthy eating. They're wholesome, light and yet full of flavour. A salad is no longer simply a side dish – an uninspired bowl of iceberg lettuce slathered with bottled dressing. It can be the star of a meal.

There is more to this book than fine recipes, however. It is also packed with information to make sophisticated eating and cooking accessible, no matter what your level of expertise. Each recipe notes preparation times, variations, serving ideas and make-ahead guidelines. For items that might seem weird as well as wonderful, I've included a guide called World Flavours. I've also demystified confusing ingredients and explored familiar ones in features on tomatoes, lettuce varieties, noodles, legumes and oils and vinegars. Most importantly, each recipe has been tested twice to guarantee that you have stunning success.

My childhood hours in a garden piqued my interest in vibrant salads. But to know the pleasures of good food, you don't need to grow it, you need spectacular new ways to prepare it. Open this book to any page and assemble a few ingredients. Then enjoy and eat well.

salad basics

Washing and Storing Salad Leaves (Greens) and Herbs

After you've chosen the crispest salad leaves (greens) and freshest herbs it is important to preserve their state as long as possible. Transport your purchases home straightaway. Any flavour will fade away with the wilted lettuce if left in a warm car. Wash them first thing to keep the freshness and revive tired leaves. Lettuces and similar plants grow close to the ground and are often awash with dirt and grit. If placed in the refrigerator without being washed and dried, they will deteriorate much faster. The best method of cleaning is in a sink full of cold water. If they are particularly wilted, add some ice to restore their vitality. Gently swish them about, drain and repeat again. To dry, drain flat on a tea towel (dishtowel) and roll up. A salad spinner can also do the job faster and more efficiently. Wrap the leaves in kitchen paper (paper towels) or a tea towel and place in a plastic bag. Store in the vegetable crisper drawer of your refrigerator. This should keep most lettuces and herbs for 2–3 days.

Essential and Nice-to-have Equipment

You won't need masses of equipment to make salads, but there are a few essential pieces that will make your life easier. Depending upon your budget and frustration factor, I've compiled "must haves" and "nice to haves". Opposite is a list that will assist you in preparing the recipes in this book with as much pleasure as possible.

Must Have

Good sharp knifes – Buy the best large chopping, small paring and serrated knives and you'll have them for a lifetime.

Vegetable peeler – Replace each year as they dull quickly.

Sharp four-sided or box grater – Excellent for grating Parmesan cheese, fresh root ginger or lemon rind.

Set of mixing bowls – Three different sizes will be particularly helpful.

Tea towels (dishtowels) – Essential for drying and wrapping leaves after washing.

Nice To Have

Salad spinner – Inexpensive and quickly dries lettuces and other leaves.

Food processor – Saves time chopping and mixing. Invest in a good brand with sharp blades and a strong motor.

Lemon squeezer – Pick your favourite: wooden reamer, glass juicer or Mexican press. Especially helpful if you like Asian lime dressings.

Mandoline – Slaws and Thai salads with large amounts of julienne or shaved vegetables are considerably easier with this. Invest in a good French or Japanese one with sharp blades. Just be careful using it.

Electronic scales – Measuring small amounts, such as 15g/½ oz, is difficult with spring scales. Electronic scales are precise and can toggle between grams and ounces.

Small whisk – Good for emulsifying thick dressings in a bowl.

Griddle pan – Although you can use a conventional grill (broiler), a griddle pan makes vegetables and meat look nicer and imparts a smoky flavour.

Mortar and pestle – Useful for making Thai Chilli Lime Dressing (see page 153) and crushing freshly toasted spices. The stone or marble varieties work best, please don't waste time and money on the ceramic type.

Electric spice grinder – Purchase an electric coffee or spice grinder to freshly grind your own spices. The taste and aroma of freshly ground spices is incomparable to the bottled variety.

Screw-top jar – The perfect vessel for mixing vinaigrettes and dressings.

Large fine strainer – Useful for rinsing noodles and lentils which will slip through a large colander.

Wok or medium heavy pan – This is essential for crispy deep-fried vegetables.

Baking (cookie) sheet or roasting pan – Practical for roasting vegetables, croûtons or meat.

Non-stick frying pan (skillet) – Invest in a good-quality make that won't chip.

world flavours

Every country around the globe has a clutch of fresh herbs, ground spices and pastes that make its cuisine unique. The French call it *je ne sais quoi* – the touch of flavour that you just can't put your finger on. These ethnic ingredients are key to what I call the "taste factor" – salads that don't just taste "okay," but are truly extraordinary. You may have to visit speciality stores, shop mail order or purchase on-line, but most of the condiments keep for a long time and are used in small quantities. Use this guide to understand these strange but wonderful gems, or gain inspiration to create your own salads.

SOUTH-EAST ASIA

Fish sauce – The salty flavouring and condiment is known as *nam pla* in Thailand and *nuoc mam* in Vietnam. Its pale liquid is produced by pressing salted fermented anchovies. It is irreplaceable in lime dressings with chillies and sugar.

Lemon grass – Its sour lemon fragrance comes from citral, an essential oil also found in lemon rind. Use the lower portion of the stem and remove the tough outer layers by crushing with a heavy knife. Finely chop the remaining tender heart. It will keep for over 1 month in the refrigerator and freezes well.

Lime leaves – The fragrant leaves from the kaffir lime tree are finely shredded for dressings or used in salads. Although fresh leaves are difficult to find, they freeze remarkably well and retain their aroma.

Palm sugar – Sometimes called jaggery, this dark, unrefined sugar is made from the boiled sap of the sugar palm tree. It is sold as a solid paste and has a caramel taste when combined with lime juice and fish sauce.

Chillies – Thanks to Christopher Columbus, the entire world now uses chillies. The general rule is the larger the chilli, the milder it is. Removing the seeds and membranes will significantly reduce the amount of heat. I would recommend using the thumb-sized variety found in supermarkets as they still impart chilli flavour but aren't packed with fire.

Ginger – Whether grated for dressings, julienned in a salad or fried for a crunchy topping, this knobbly root lends a pungent aroma that is both sweet and peppery.

Sweet chilli dipping sauce – This gooey, sweet and spicy condiment is normally used for dipping fried delicacies or grilled (broiled) meat, but is sometimes added to dressings.

Coconut milk or cream – Combine with fish sauce, lime juice and sugar to make a creamy dressing for prawns (shrimp) or shredded chicken. When opening a can of coconut milk, scoop out the solid portion for cream or shake the can first to mix and use as milk.

Fresh herbs – Mint, coriander (cilantro) and sweet basil feature often and are used as whole leaves rather than chopped, adding vivid taste and colour.

Thai sweet basil – This aromatic herb with small pointy leaves is similar to Mediterranean basil, but more liquorice in flavour. Sold only in Thai stores, it should not be confused with holy basil, which is used in curries. It goes off quickly so use within 2 days of purchasing.

MEDITERRANEAN

Capers – Valued for their sharp taste in dressings and salads, capers are actually the small flower buds of a Mediterranean bush. The small salt-packed variety is preferable to the brined. Rinse well or soak before using to remove the salt. They are wonderful when combined with anchovies and garlic.

Caper berries – Mostly used in Spanish tapas or salads, these delicious bites are actually large capers. Left on the bush slightly longer than capers, they develop a seedy centre similar to a fig. They are sold in brine and should be stored in the refrigerator.

Olives – Grown mostly in the Mediterranean, South America and the United States, there are dozens of varieties. My favourite is the black dry-cured Italian variety, which is not overly dominant and easy to pit. Excellent puréed in dressings or chopped in salads.

Anchovies – You either love or hate them, but these tiny Mediterranean fish are coveted for their salty piquant taste. Sold in jars or cans, packed in salt or olive oil. The Spanish or Italian brands are the best quality. Rinse well, then soak in milk or water for 5 minutes to remove the strong fishy taste.

Saba – Similar to verjuice, this is a non-alcoholic liquid made from concentrated grape juice. Excellent for plumping up dried fruit with balsamic vinegar or used in dressings.

Fennel seeds – Not to be confused with aniseed (anise seed), fennel tastes like liquorice, but sweeter. Lovely when coarsely ground for dressings, it complements pork or seafood salads.

Oregano – This herb is similar to marjoram, but with a stronger, more pungent aroma. Used in small amounts both fresh and dried, it is very distinctive in salads. The dried Mexican variety is extremely strong, so be frugal.

Fresh herbs – Flat leaf or Italian parsley, dill, oregano, mint, basil, thyme, chives and tarragon feature strongly in the Mediterranean. All lend a clean herbaceous taste that is beguiling in vinaigrettes or mixed with vegetables and lettuce.

LATIN AND SOUTH AMERICAN

Chipotles in adobo sauce – Fiery reconstituted dried chillies packed in a garlicky tomato sauce and usually sold in cans. They start out their life as jalapeño chillies and are then smoked while dried. It's this process that imparts their smoky flavour. They are lovely in potato salads or combined with lime juice for a spicy dressing.

Jalapeño chillies – There are more than 200 varieties of chillies and over 100 are from Mexico. With so many to choose from, it can be overwhelming. For salads, stick with the jalapeño or common thumb-sized green

chilli found at most supermarkets. Remove the seeds and membranes to lessen the heat. Green chillies are particularly good in dressings with lime and coriander (cilantro).

Chilli powder – The types of chillies used in this will vary, but most will have a spicy-smoky flavour. It works well in tomato, sweet lettuce or potato salads.

Paprika – Both the Hungarian and Spanish pimentón varieties could be used, depending on your taste. The Spanish will be smokier in flavour. Most paprika loses its fragrance after 6 months, so be sure to replace regularly.

Cayenne pepper – This extremely hot ground spice is made from bright red chillies with the same name. A little goes a long way and it is used sparingly for a touch of heat.

Fresh herbs – Coriander (cilantro) is the major herb used in Mexico and most Latin American cooking. It's used in almost everything.

MIDDLE EASTERN AND NORTH AFRICAN

Pomegranate molasses – This syrupy Persian condiment is produced from the concentrated juice of the world's most labour-intensive fruit – the pomegranate. Its exotic sweet and sour taste makes delectable dressings. It is a useful alternative to vinegar.

Preserved lemon – Lemons are packed in a salt and lemon juice mixture that removes the bitterness and instils a sweet taste. Not only used for tagines, they are also excellent chopped up in North African salads. All the flesh should be removed, and the rind thoroughly rinsed before using. To make your own, place 5 quartered lemons in a jar with 80 g/3 oz/½ cup sea salt. Cover with lemon juice, seal with a lid and leave for 2 weeks.

Harissa - This spicy chilli paste from North Africa and the Middle East is sold in small jars or tubes. The fiery hot sauce is usually made with chillies, garlic, cumin, coriander and olive oil. Use it in small amounts for spice and a touch of heat.

Greek (strained plain) yogurt – The aristocrat of yogurt, this creamy, full-fat (whole) yogurt has been strained, providing a thick texture similar to crème fraîche. It is lovely for dressings used on cucumbers, couscous or roasted vegetable salads. If you can't find it, strain another full-fat yogurt overnight through muslin (cheesecloth).

Pimentón paprika – Very different from Hungarian paprika, the Spanish variety is characteristically smoky. Moroccan carrots and other Spanish and North African salads come alive with this noble, cherry-coloured spice. It's sold in little cans as picante or dulce, depending on your heat preference.

Sumac – This purple-hued Lebanese spice is ground from the berries of the sumac tree. It has a sour, astringent taste and is used to sprinkle on salads or cheeses. Fattoush, the chopped Middle Eastern salad with toasted pitta, is where it most commonly appears.

Saffron – This is the world's most expensive spice. Orange-red stigmas provide wondrous colour and flavour for couscous, chicken or garlic aioli. Buy the threads instead of powder, which could be adulterated with other spices. To maximize its potential, crush the saffron with the bowl of a spoon and infuse (steep) with a tablespoon of hot water before using.

Cumin – An ancient spice, this is nutty in flavour and works well with poultry, seafood and couscous salads. There is a world of difference between buying it already ground and toasting and grinding the seeds yourself. It's best to buy in small quantities and use frequently. The fragrance is lost after about 6 months.

Coriander – Another ancient spice, this dates back to Egyptian times. It complements salads with meat, chicken or roasted (bell) peppers. Buy fresh seeds every 6 months and try to toast and grind them yourself rather than buying already ground.

Cinnamon – Harvested from the inner bark of a tropical evergreen tree, this spice is sold in sticks or ground. There are two varieties: Ceylon is light coloured and sweet, while Cassia, a dark, red-brown colour, has more pungent bittersweet flavour. It is lovely for couscous or poultry salads with pomegranate syrup.

Fresh herbs – Some salads in the Middle East have more herbs than lettuce or vegetables. Flat leaf parsley, coriander (cilantro), mint and dill are the workhorses here and are used frequently.

INDIAN

Cardamom – An aromatic spice, with a warm, sweet taste, cardamom can be purchased either in the pod or ground. Most of the ground selection lacks flavour as the seeds lose their essential oils quickly. Use a mortar and pestle to crush the shell, remove the seeds and finely grind them. Since it's used in small quantities, it won't be too much work.

Turmeric – With its intense yellow-orange hue, turmeric is coveted for its flavour and colour. It works well in potato or chicken salads. Discard after 6 months as the aroma will fade quickly.

Mustard seeds – These tiny, pearl-like seeds suit dressings on potato, coleslaw or other hearty salads. Toast lightly before using.

Coriander – See MIDDLE EASTERN AND NORTH AFRICAN above.

Cumin – See MIDDLE EASTERN AND NORTH AFRICAN above.

Curry powder – Indians make their own freshly ground supply every day, so you can imagine what they think of our commercial brands. A pulverized assortment of up to 20 spices, curry powder has hundreds of variations. 'Masala' means mixture; each region of India has its own special blend with different names such as Madras or garam masala. It's simple to make your own with an electric spice grinder and the difference is enormous.

Desiccated (dry unsweetened shredded) coconut – This is made from dehydrated shredded coconut. Use the non-sweetened type for fruit or vegetable salads. It is very popular in South-east Asian cooking as well as Indian.

Fresh herbs – Coriander (cilantro), curry leaves, dill and mint are widely used.

CHINESE

Soy sauce – An important ingredient for all Asian cooking, this is made by fermenting, boiled soya beans and roasted wheat or barley. There are many varieties, ranging from thin to very thick, and they will be labelled as such. Light soy sauce is thinner and saltier and dark soy sauce is thicker but not so salty. Unless a recipe calls for a specific type just use regular "soy sauce."

Chinese rice wine – This is a cooking and drinking wine made from millet, rice and yeast. It has a flavour that is similar to dry sherry, which could be used as a substitute if necessary. Shaohsing is said to be the best quality. It is good in soy-based dressings for fried vegetables such as aubergines (eggplant) or green beans.

Hoisin sauce – This reddish brown sauce tastes sweet and sour. Most brands consist of soya bean paste, sugar, garlic and vinegar. It is best used for noodle, duck and chicken salads.

Chilli bean paste – This zippy sauce is noted for its spicy, salty and sour taste. Made with fermented soya beans or black beans, dried chillies, garlic and other seasonings, it works well in noodle salad dressings.

Ginger and chillies – See SOUTH-EAST ASIAN above.

Fresh herbs – Coriander (cilantro) and chives are most prevalent.

JAPANESE

Pickled ginger – Slices of young root ginger are preserved in sweet vinegar. It is a tasty ingredient in salads, dressings or as a beautiful garnish.

Nori – This seaweed is predominately used a sushi wrapper, but its sweet ocean taste makes it great for slicing on Japanese or rice salads. It is extremely rich in vitamins, minerals, and protein.

Mirin – Sometimes referred to as Japanese sweet sake, mirin is rice wine with added sugar. It adds a subtle sweetness to soy dressings.

Miso paste – A savoury fermented soya bean paste and seasoning, this lends a nutty salty taste. There are four varieties: white (rice) mild tasting; yellow (rice) saltier and more tart; red (barley) deep flavour; and dark brown (beans) rich and much saltier. It keeps in the refrigerator for 3 months.

Wasabi paste – A fiercely hot Japanese horseradish paste, this is traditionally eaten with sushi. One small taste can clear your nasal passage in seconds, so it should be used sparingly. Adds an interesting touch of heat to Asian and Japanese dressings for noodles or seared fish salads. It is sold as a powder or ready-mixed in a tube.

Tamari – This is a wheat-free soy sauce. Some consider its flavour to be more subtle or mellower than Chinese soy sauce. It is excellent in soy dressings.

Sesame seeds – The first recorded seasoning in history goes all the way back to 3000 BC. These tiny, flat seeds come in different shades, the most common being pale ivory and black. When toasted, they gain a nutty, oily taste and are tremendous tossed over Asian salads. Black sesame seeds are dramatic for coating and searing chicken or seafood for salads.

INDONESIAN

Kecap manis – This intensely dark brown, syrupy sauce is similar to soy, but sweeter and more complex. It is made with soy, palm sugar, garlic and star anise. Its thick sweet disposition is ideal for coating noodles or used in other Asian dressings with chilli, garlic and ginger.

Sambal oelek – This paste made from chillies, brown sugar and salt is usually found small jars. Perfect for lazy days when you don't feel like chopping fresh chillies, it is excellent in soy- and lime-based dressings.

Tamarind – One of the secret ingredients in Worcestershire sauce and Coca Cola, tamarind has a sour-sweet taste. It is made from the pulp taken from the large pods of an Indian tree. The sticky paste is soaked in hot water, strained and then used for iced drinks, dressings and sauces. It is found in Asian food stores in sticky chunks or as a liquid in jars.

Fresh herbs– Many of the same herbs are popular throughout South-east Asia; coriander (cilantro), basil, mint and lemon grass are used frequently.

salad leaves (greens)

Salad leaves (greens) are the backbone for most salads, adding texture, subtle taste and glorious colour. A bonus is that they have an abundance of nutrition and contain few calories. The general rule is, the darker the colour, the more health it contains. Most are rich in vitamins A and C, but some, such as spinach, contain iron. Growing your own couldn't be easier, but if a green thumb evades you, there is a huge selection available to buy. These days, supermarkets are steadfastly introducing new lettuces and baby leaves. Your excitement can rapidly turn to confusion owing to the myriad of varieties. Don't feel overwhelmed – use the groupings in this guide to identify what you want.

MILD LEAVES

These sweet and subtle leaves are featured too often in the ubiquitous tossed green salad. They desperately aspire to move on to a more sophisticated life. Strong flavours were made for these leaves. Piquant cheeses, such as feta, Parmesan and Gorgonzola, pair well, along with garlicky vinaigrettes and creamy dressings. Delicate round lettuce is ideal for South-east Asian salads with their tasty lime-chilli dressing. Spinach and Cos and romaine lettuces are the workhorses of this group. Their strong texture keeps well once they have been dressed.

Red oak leaf lettuce (8)

Lollo rosso

Lollo biondo (9)

Round (butterhead)

Boston

Iceberg (crisphead)

Lamb's lettuce (mâche)

Spinach

Cos lettuce/romaine lettuce

Little Gem (Bibb) lettuce

SPICY–PEPPERY LEAVES

Velvety soft in texture, but spicy in taste, peppery leaves are perfect for flavourful olive oils and vinegars, citrus vinaigrettes, Asian soy and garlicky dressings. Combine a couple of varieties rather than using just one alone. They also work extremely well mixed with mild lettuces or bitter leaves, such as chicory (Belgian endive). Most often, you'll fine the baby leaves sold together as mesclun. This mixture is usually made up of baby chard, baby mustard leaves, rocket (arugula) and mizuna. Sophisticated and full of taste, mesclun can make an excellent salad on its own with a simple vinaigrette. For added glamour, try adding edible flowers, such as nasturtiums.

Watercress

Rocket (arugula)

Mizuna (1)

Baby kale

Tatsoi

Baby mustard leaves (2)

Baby beetroot tops (beet greens) (3)

Baby chard

BITTER LEAVES

Prized for their lovely texture and unique bitter taste, these hearty leaves cry out for counterparts such as toasted nuts, fried pancetta, and blue cheese. Magnificent when dressed with raspberry, sherry and balsamic vinegars, nut oils and warm vinaigrettes with garlic and anchovies. Frisée is essential for French salads with warm goat's cheese, poached eggs or crunchy bacon. Radicchio is crucial to the Italians' *insalata mista*, and its vivid red brightens up otherwise dull colours. Don't just stop at serving these leaves raw, they are superb when grilled (broiled) or braised.

Radicchio (6)

Treviso

Chicory (Belgian endive) (7)

Frisée/curly endive

Escarole

Dandelion leaves

CABBAGES

These ubiquitous green vegetables have sadly endured a downtrodden reputation. Not only to be enjoyed in economic downturns, they make the most colourful, crunchy and delicious salads. Unlike most salad leaves, they can sit in the dressing for days without relinquishing their texture. Coleslaws and warm winter salads are where they're used most. Crisp, raw chopped vegetables, such as onions, (bell) peppers and carrots make lovely additions. Dressings can range from tangy mayonnaise-based to tart vinaigrettes with celery or caraway seeds. Chinese cabbage is best for Asian coleslaws featuring rice wine vinegar and sesame seed oil.

Savoy

White

Green

Red (5)

Chinese leaves (Napa cabbage/Chinese cabbage) (4)

in the beginning –
antipasti, mezze and tapas 1

Diminutive in size but colossal in taste, mezze, antipasti or tapas are the inauguration to a meal. Dazzling flavours tease your taste buds, warming up the palate for more. Sharp cheeses, sweet peppers or salty anchovies can all be fashioned into these up-market snacks eaten with a fork, fingers or a piece of bread. Not surprisingly, they can be the most memorable part of lunch or dinner.

balsamic fig, prosciutto and ricotta crostini
with rocket (arugula) salad

My great friend Victoria and I ate this delicious salad at an Italian trattoria in Toronto. We couldn't wait to replicate it at home. Middle Eastern stores sell miniature figs or other high-quality dried ones.

SERVES 6 (APPETIZER), 4 (MAIN COURSE) OR 8 (SIDE DISH)

PREPARATION TIME: 30 MINUTES

16 dried good-quality figs

125 ml/4 fl oz/½ cup balsamic vinegar, plus extra for drizzling

125 ml/4 fl oz/½ cup water

1 tbsp sugar

1 tsp salt

½ tsp freshly ground black pepper, plus extra for serving

2 large handfuls of rocket (arugula)

100 g/3½ oz/scant ½ cup full-fat ricotta cheese

8 slices toasted ciabatta, sourdough or French bread, brushed with olive oil

8 slices prosciutto

Place the figs in a small pan, add water to cover and bring to the boil, then lower the heat and simmer for 10 minutes. Drain.

Bring the balsamic vinegar and measured water to the boil with the sugar, salt and pepper. Add the figs, lower the heat and simmer for 15 minutes or until vinegar is syrupy and the figs are reconstituted. Leave to cool slightly. Arrange the rocket (arugula) on individual plates or a large dish. Spread the ricotta over each piece of toasted bread, then place a slice of prosciutto on the cheese. Top each crostini with 2 sliced figs and arrange on the rocket.

Drizzle a little extra balsamic vinegar over the salad. Grind black pepper over everything and serve.

GET ORGANIZED

Toast the bread 2 days ahead. Prepare the figs the day before and reheat before making salad. The crostini should not be assembled until just before serving.

VARIATIONS

Substitute goat's cheese or Gorgonzola for ricotta. Fresh figs can replace the dried, but marinate with balsamic vinegar and don't heat through.

roasted baby courgettes (zucchini),
mint and bocconcini with warm agrodolce vinaigrette

SERVES 6 (APPETIZER) OR 8 (SIDE DISH)

PREPARATION TIME: 30 MINUTES

600 g/1 lb 5 oz baby courgettes (zucchini), halved lengthways or 6 small courgettes, cut into 1 cm/½ inch slices lengthways

6 tbsp olive oil

1 tsp salt

1 tsp freshly ground black pepper

150 g/5 oz bocconcini mozzarella (baby mozzarella) cheeses or 3 standard mozzarella cheeses cut into 2.5 cm/1 inch chunks

25 fresh mint leaves

FOR THE SWEET AND SOUR VINAIGRETTE

5 tbsp extra virgin olive oil

2 garlic cloves, thinly sliced

5 tbsp red wine vinegar

½ tsp crushed red chilli

1½ tbsp clear honey

1 small red onion, thinly sliced

1 tsp salt

1 tsp freshly ground black pepper

I tried this recipe many times and couldn't quite get it right. I rang my friend Ursula Ferrigno, a fabulous Italian cook, to find out why. "Never use courgettes wider than your thumb," she told me. The results, using slim courgettes complemented by baby mozzarella and bathed in a warm, sweet and sour vinaigrette, were finally exquisite.

Heat oven to 200°C/400°F/Gas mark 6.

Place the courgettes (zucchini) in a shallow roasting pan and toss with the olive oil, salt and pepper. Roast, shaking the pan every 10 minutes to prevent sticking, for 20–30 minutes until they are golden brown. Remove from oven and place on a platter.

For the sweet and sour vinaigrette. Heat the olive oil and garlic in a small pan until the garlic is golden. Add the vinegar, chilli, honey and onion, season with the salt and pepper and simmer for 4–5 minutes until the mixture is syrupy. Remove from the heat and set aside.

Arrange the cheese over the courgettes. Drizzle the vinaigrette over the salad and sprinkle with the mint leaves. Serve warm or at room temperature.

GET ORGANIZED

The salad can be prepared 3 hours in advance. If left longer, the flavours can become too strong.

VARIATIONS

Lemon, balsamic or red wine vinaigrettes could replace the sweet and sour vinaigrette. You can chargrill the courgettes (zucchini) instead of roasting them. Feta, Gorgonzola or ricotta cheese could replace the mozarella.

roasted red (bell) peppers
with honey and pine nuts

What don't roasted (bell) peppers taste good with? Virtually any dressing complements them but this is one of my favourites. The sweetness of the peppers melds beautifully with honey and balsamic vinegar. Roasting your own is easy and is worth the effort.

SERVES 4-6 (APPETIZER) OR 8 (SIDE DISH)

PREPARATION TIME: 20 MINUTES

8 red and/or yellow (bell) peppers, de-seeded and cut into quarters

4 tbsp extra virgin olive oil

2 large garlic cloves, thinly sliced

2 tbsp balsamic vinegar

3 tbsp chopped fresh flat leaf parsley

60 g/2 oz/½ cup pine nuts

2 tbsp clear honey

1 tsp salt

1 tsp freshly ground black pepper

Heat the grill (broiler). Place the (bell) peppers, skin side up, on a large baking (cookie) sheet. Grill (broil) until blackened, then place in a plastic bag, seal and set aside for 5 minutes.

When the peppers are cool enough to handle, remove the skins, but do not rinse. Chop the flesh into 1 cm/½ inch pieces and place in a medium bowl.

Heat the olive oil in a sauté pan and cook the garlic until golden. Pour the mixture over the peppers and add the vinegar, parsley, pine nuts, honey, salt and pepper. Mix well and leave at room temperature.

GET ORGANIZED

The (bell) peppers can be fully prepared and will keep for 2 days in the refrigerator.

VARIATIONS

Feta cheese or chunks of Gorgonzola can be added. For Spanish tapas, substitute sherry vinegar for the balsamic. For a Middle Eastern flavour, replace the vinegar with fresh lemon juice and add chopped fresh mint and harissa. For a substantial salad, serve Sicilian pork sausages or grilled chicken sliced on top.

smoky aubergines (eggplant)
with tomatoes and dill

Although the method can seem a little chaotic, the secret to this delectable salad is to blacken the aubergine (eggplant) over a hob (stovetop) flame. This imparts a magical smokiness – exquisite when combined with garlic, spring onion (scallion) and dill. Serve with warm pitta bread or crunchy Cos or romaine lettuce leaves.

Pierce the whole, unpeeled aubergines (eggplant) with the point of a knife in several places. Using tongs, hold each aubergine over an open flame on the hob (stovetop). Turn each one as it blackens and continue until it is charred all over. Alternatively, grill on a barbecue or under a conventional grill (broiler). Place in a colander to drain off any excess liquid.

When the aubergines are cool enough to handle, carefully peel off the black skins and cut off the stalks. Remove any large seeds and chop coarsely. Transfer to large bowl.

Add the tomatoes, onion, garlic, spring onions (scallions), olive oil, lemon juice, parsley and dill. Season with salt and pepper and gently combine.

SERVES 6 (APPETIZER) OR 8 (SIDE DISH)

PREPARATION TIME: 20 MINUTES.

3 large firm aubergines (eggplant)

2 large ripe plum tomatoes, de-seeded and diced

1 small red onion, finely chopped

3 garlic cloves, finely chopped

4 spring onions (scallions), thinly sliced

4 tbsp olive oil

1 tbsp fresh lemon juice

1 tbsp finely chopped fresh flat leaf parsley

1 tbsp finely chopped fresh dill

1 tsp salt

1 tsp freshly ground black pepper

GET ORGANIZED

The salad can be prepared 2 hours in advance, but don't add the onions until just before seving.

VARIATIONS

Mix 7 tbsp Greek (plain, strained) yogurt or 100g/3½ oz soft goat's cheese through the salad. Add other herbs. such as mint or fresh coriander (cilantro). Mix in ½ tsp ground allspice or cinnamon for an exotic flavour.

Egyptian feta salad
with dill and mint

Claudia Roden's time-honoured recipes burst with magical flavour and pure health tastes. This salad was inspired by her book, *The New Book of Middle Eastern Food*. Be sure to use creamy Greek or Turkish feta cheese as domestic varieties can be too salty. Dried dill is completely out of the question.

Crumble the feta into a bowl and mash with the oil and lemon juice. Season with black pepper.

Add the cucumber, onion and chopped herbs and mix gently. Season with salt if necessary.

Serve with crunchy strips of pitta bread (see recipe for Pitta Croûtons on page 156, cutting the bread into long strips rather than cubes).

SERVES 6 (APPETIZER) OR 8 (SIDE DISH)

PREPARATION TIME: 10 MINUTES

200 g/7 oz feta cheese, drained

3 tbsp extra virgin olive oil

juice of ½ lemon

1/2 tsp black pepper

2 small Lebanese cucumbers, trimmed and diced, or 1 medium cucumber, de-seeded and diced.

1 small red onion, finely diced

2 tbsp chopped fresh mint

2 tbsp chopped fresh parsley

2 tbsp chopped fresh dill

salt (optional)

pitta bread, to serve

GET ORGANIZED

This salad can be partially assembled 3 hours beforehand, but add the lemon, olive oil, and red onion just before serving.

VARIATION

Add ½ tsp ground cumin for a subtle spicy flavour or 1 finely diced red chilli. Substitute hard goat's cheese for the feta.

caponata

SERVES 6 (APPETIZER),
4 (MAIN COURSE) OR
8 (SIDE DISH)

PREPARATION TIME:
45 MINUTES

3 medium aubergines
(eggplant), unpeeled and cut
into 3 cm/1¼ inch pieces

125 ml/4 fl oz/½ cup olive oil

1 tsp each salt and
black pepper

1 large onion, chopped into
1 cm/½ inch pieces

1 red (bell) pepper,
de-seeded and chopped
into 1 cm/½ inch pieces

6 celery sticks, cut into
1 cm/½ inch pieces

125 ml/4 fl oz/½ cup white
wine vinegar

1 tbsp tomato purée (paste)

2 tbsp capers, rinsed

15 green olives, pitted
and rinsed

2 tbsp caster (superfine) sugar

FOR THE TOMATO SAUCE

3 tbsp olive oil

1 anchovy rinsed

3 garlic cloves,
finely chopped

2 x 400f/14 oz cans
good-quality plum
tomatoes, puréed

½ tsp each of salt and
black pepper

Heat the oven to 200°C/400°F/Gas Mark 6.

Place the aubergine (eggplant) pieces on a large baking (cookie) sheet, drizzle 4 tbsp of the olive oil over them, sprinkle with half the salt and pepper and mix. Bake, shaking the baking sheet occasionally to prevent sticking, for 20 minutes or until golden brown. Set aside.

For the tomato sauce: Heat the olive oil in a medium pan. Add the anchovy and garlic and sauté until the garlic is golden. Add the tomatoes, salt and pepper and stir well. Cook over a medium-high heat for 15 minutes until thickened and reduced, then set aside.

Heat the remaining olive oil in a large sauté pan. Add the onion, (bell) pepper, celery and remaining salt and pepper and sauté for 5 minutes until slightly soft, but still firm. Add the vinegar, tomato purée (paste), capers, olives and tomato sauce and cook for 5 minutes. Remove from the heat and leave to cool.

GET ORGANIZED

The entire salad can be made up to 4 days in advance and the flavour is actually better after 24 hours.

VARIATIONS

Top with grilled swordfish, tuna or thin slices of chicken breast.

Moroccan carrots

This classic North African carrot salad is like a breath of fresh air with its zesty vinaigrette of paprika, parsley and garlic. Make it elegant by using whole baby carrots or slice them into batons or coins. It is a great addition for mezze or eaten slightly mashed with pitta bread.

Mix together the olive oil, vinegar, paprika, cumin, garlic, parsley, salt and pepper in a medium bowl.

Cook carrots in salted, boiling water until they are tender but still firm. Overcooking will produce a slimy texture so drain them immediately they are al dente.

Toss the carrots with vinaigrette and leave at room temperature until ready to serve or chill overnight.

SERVES 6 (APPETIZER) OR 8 (SIDE DISH)

PREPARATION TIME: 20 MINUTES

125 ml/4 fl oz/½ cup extra virgin olive oil

6 tbsp Cabernet Sauvignon red wine vinegar

2 tsp sweet paprika (preferably pimentón)

2 tsp ground cumin

3 garlic cloves, finely chopped

1 handful of fresh flat leaf parsley, finely chopped

1 tsp salt

½ tsp freshly ground black pepper

750g/1 lb 10 oz whole baby carrots, trimmed or organic carrots, trimmed, peeled and sliced into 1 cm/½ inch slices or batons.

GET ORGANIZED

Make the entire salad 24 hours in advance and store in the refrigerator.

VARIATIONS

Substitute Classic Red Wine Vinaigrette (see page 150) for the dressing to make an Italian antipasto.

Spanish tapas – piquillo peppers stuffed with goat's cheese, saffron patatas aioli and asparagus with sherry vinaigrette

Tapas are not just a snack, but distinctive meals on their own. Ranging from leeks in vinaigrette to a humble seared chorizo sausage, all are blessed with robust flavours. Accompanied by a glass of chilled sherry – this is my idea of how food should be eaten. Piquillo are tiny red peppers that are smoked as well as roasted. You will find them in sold in jars along with other fantastic ingredients at Spanish food stores.

SERVES 6 (APPETIZER) OR 4 MAIN COURSE

PREPARATION TIME: 60 MINUTES

FOR THE PIQUILLO PEPPERS STUFFED WITH GOAT'S CHEESE

200 g/7 oz hard goats cheese

2 x 200 g/7 oz/1 cup jars piquillo peppers, drained

2 tbsp finely chopped fresh parsley

½ tsp each salt and freshly ground black pepper

FOR THE SAFFRON PATATAS AIOLI

6 large red potatoes (Maris Piper preferably)

1 quantity Saffron Aioli (see page 150)

1 large bunch of fresh chives, finely chopped

FOR THE ASPARAGUS WITH SHERRY VINAIGRETTE

2 bunches of asparagus, trimmed

2 tbsp finely chopped fresh parsley

1 quantity Sherry and Olive Oil Vinaigrette (see page 150)

For the Piquillo Peppers Stuffed with Goat's Cheese: Slice the cheese into 1 cm/ ½ inch pieces and gently stuff it into peppers. Sprinkle with the parsley and season with the salt and pepper. Chill in the refrigerator until required.

For the Saffron Patatas Aioli: Cook the unpeeled potatoes in salted, boiling water until tender. Drain and leave to cool slightly, then peel potatoes and cut into 1 cm/ ½ inch cubes.

Prepare dressing and mix gently with the cubed potatoes. Sprinkle with chopped chives and chill in the refrigerator until required.

For the Asparagus with Sherry Vinaigrette: Blanch the asparagus in salted, boiling water until al dente. Drain and immediately immerse in iced water for 2 minutes. Dry on kitchen paper (paper towels). Pour some of the vinaigrette over it and set aside.

To serve: Arrange all tapas on a large platter or plate individually. Spoon a small amount of the remaining Sherry Vinaigrette over the Piquillo Peppers.

GET ORGANIZED

All dishes can be prepared and refrigerated up to 5 hours ahead.

VARIATIONS

You can change all of these dishes to have an Italian feel by substituting red wine or balsamic vinaigrette. Ricotta or other Italian cheeses can be used for stuffing the piquillo peppers. If you can't get piquillo peppers, then use regular roasted (bell) peppers halved, stuffed and rolled.

using your bean and lentils and grains too

2

A nutritional powerhouse, beans and grains are universally enjoyed by different cultures around the world. Regardless of whether it's Puy lentils, creamy borlotti beans or chewy bulgar wheat, their filling, starchy texture can satisfy like no other food. Left on their own, they are a blank canvas. But give them some fresh herbs, bacon or vinegar and they start to become a work of art.

pod power

Packed with vitamins and fibre, beans and lentils are astonishingly good for you. They provide a wonderful foundation for salads, soaking up the tangy flavours. Legumes, also called pulses, are seeds or beans which come from a pod. Sometimes lentils are referred to as *dhal*, an Indian word meaning split pulse. Lentils can be boiled quickly, but beans require soaking before cooking. Although cans are quick and easy, boiling dried beans preserves the texture and nutritional content. Cover with water the night before, drain and simmer in fresh water for 30 minutes up to 2 hours until soft. Don't add salt until the last 10 minutes of cooking. Look for legumes that are shiny and uniform in size and colour. Store for up to 6 months in a dark cool place.

BEANS

Cannellini (1) – Large oval beans with a creamy, mild flavour. Use in Mediterranean salads with tomatoes, fresh herbs and balsamic vinaigrettes.

Borlotti/cranberry/tongue of fire (2) – Plump, beige/burgundy-striped bean, with a smooth texture and mild taste. Loves garlic, olive oil, pancetta, tomatoes or any other Italian-style ingredients.

Haricot/great northern/navy (3) – These are all members of the white bean family and are small to medium in size. Although they could be swapped for cannellini in salads, their ordinary taste is better suited to stews.

Flageolets (6) – A creamy oval bean that is actually an immature kidney bean. It's lovely moss-green colour is retained after boiling. It is excellent with olive oil and fresh herbs.

Broad/fava – Predominately eaten fresh instead of dried in salads. The tough, outer skin of both these beans needs to be removed before using. Like the artichoke, they are a labour of love to peel and prepare. Sharp cheeses, such as pecorino (romano) or pungent goat's cheese, suit them well.

Chickpeas/garbanzo beans (4) – Universally loved for their nutty flavour and creamy texture, these round, crinkled beans are extremely versatile for any combination of herbs, spices, yogurt, cheeses or spiky vinaigrettes.

Black eyed beans/peas – Round and white with a purple bulls-eye spot, they look interesting and make unusual salads. Their sweet taste, and starchy texture are best complemented by fried bacon, greens and a cider or sherry vinegar dressing.

Red kidney – Long associated with "three bean salad", this big red bean is capable of much greater things with its richness and meaty texture. Cumin, cider vinegar, chillies and other strong Latin American ingredients work nicely with them.

Aduki/adzuki – Imported from Japan, these are small maroon beans with a white stripe. Nutty and sweet with a creamy texture, they partner well with crunchy vegetables, tofu (beancurd) and Asian or citrus dressings.

Black (5) – Sometimes referred to as turtle beans, these little purple/black pulses have a delicious earthiness. Perfect in salads involving fresh coriander (cilantro), tomatoes, mango, corn, cumin and lime or cider vinegar dressings.

Mung beans (7) – Tiny green pulses with yellow centres, these can be ground to make cellophane noodles, or split into *dhal* (moong dhal). Delicious with sharp dressings and salty cheeses.

Pinto/rattlesnake/appaloosa – These are all from the red kidney bean family, but are slightly smaller and oval shaped. They share a creamy texture, strong beany flavour and lovely pale brown colouring. Their "cowboy" names refer to their unusual decorations; rattlesnakes adorned with dark-brown veins, pintos with speckled white spots and appaloosas with black/brown spots. Use in salads with smoky chipotle chillies, feta, lots of fresh coriander (cilantro) and strong sherry or cider vinegars.

LENTILS

Red (9) – Very small and delicate lentil with an orange-red hue. Works well with cumin, roasted vegetables, feta or goat's cheese, fresh herbs and citrus dressings.

Yellow – Also referred to as pigeon or gunga peas, they have a wonderful yellow colour, but a soft texture. Use with Indian flavours, such as yogurt, cumin and lemon.

Green and brown – The largest of the lentils, they both have good flavour. Unfortunately, they do not hold their texture well after cooking and become slightly mushy. Preferably use Puy when available.

Puy (8) – Small green and silver-flecked lentils sourced from the French region of Le Puy. Valued for their firm texture, they are unquestionably the best lentils for salads. There are similar lentils from Umbria, Italy, which are green/brown and of excellent quality. They work well with any ingredients: yogurt, curry spice, vinaigrettes, roasted (bell) peppers, sausage, or goat's cheese.

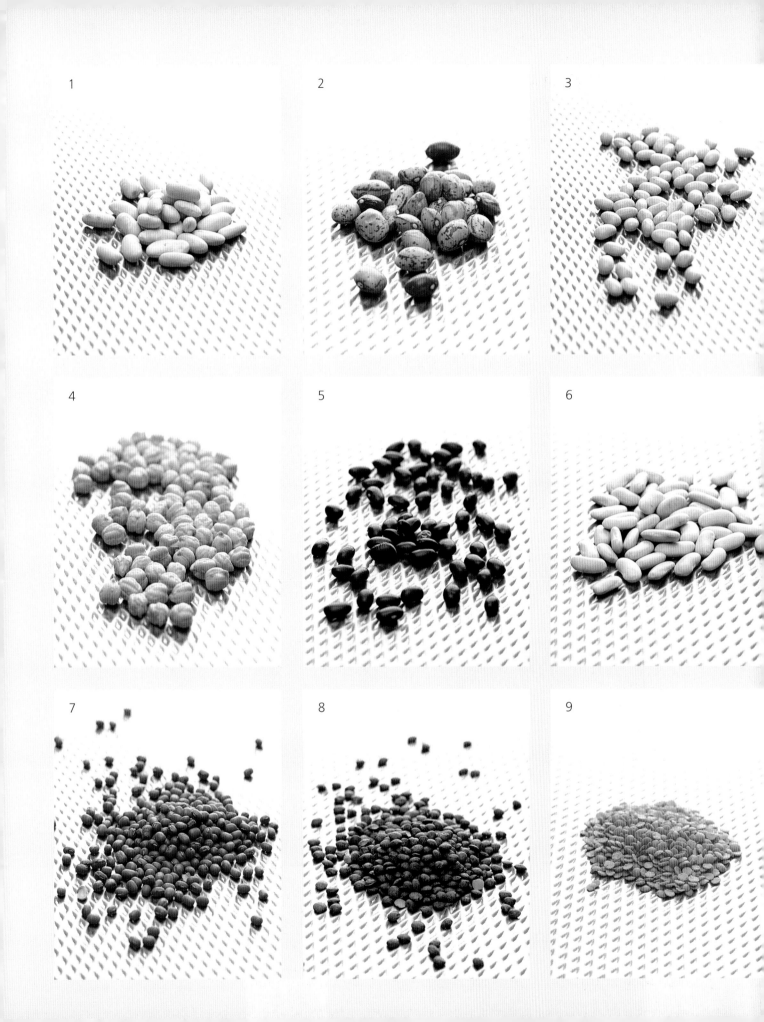

1

2

3

4

5

6

7

8

9

chickpea (garbanzo bean),
chilli and feta salad

These ingredients make a fabulous salad with exotic Middle Eastern flavours. Pomegranate syrup, a reduction of pomegranate juice, is the magic elixir in this recipe.

Pour the dressing ingredients into a screw-top jar, shake well and set aside.

Combine chickpeas (garbanzo beans), chillies, cucumbers, onion, mint, coriander (cilantro), cumin seeds and salt and pepper in a large bowl.

Just before serving, pour the dressing over the salad and sprinkle with the crumbled feta.

SERVES 6 (APPETIZER), 4 (MAIN COURSE) OR 8 (SIDE DISH)

PREPARATION TIME: 20 MINUTES

1 quantity Pomegranate Dressing (see page 150) or Lemon and Olive Oil Dressing (see page 152)

2 x 400 g/14 oz cans chickpeas (garbanzo beans), drained and rinsed, or 250 g/8 oz/1¼ cups dried chickpeas, soaked overnight and boiled for 1 hour

3 red chillies, de-seeded and finely chopped

3 Lebanese cucumbers, finely diced, or 1 medium cucumber, de-seeded and diced

1 large red onion, finely chopped

15 g/½ oz/½ cup fresh mint, finely chopped

15 g/½ oz/½ cup fresh coriander (cilantro), finely chopped

1 tsp cumin seeds

1 tsp each salt and black pepper

200 g/7 oz feta cheese, crumbled

GET ORGANIZED

The salad and dressing can be prepared 6 hours before, but don't add the dressing, cheese or onions until just before serving.

VARIATIONS

Pitted olives, thinly sliced chicken breast or lamb could be added. Classic Red Wine Vinaigrette (see page 150) dressing could be used as alternative dressing.

chickpea (garbanzo bean), chorizo and pepper salad with sherry vinegar dressing

SERVES 6 (APPETIZER),
4 (MAIN COURSE) OR
8 (SIDE DISH)

PREPARATION TIME:
30 MINUTES

450 g/1 lb fresh chorizo
sausage, cut into ½ inch slices

1 quantity Sherry and Olive
Oil Vinaigrette (see page 150)

2 x 400 g/14 oz cans
chickpeas (garbanzo beans),
drained and rinsed, or
250 g/8 oz/1¼ cups dried
chickpeas, soaked overnight
and boiled for 1-2 hours
or until soft

200 g/7 oz piquillo or other
roasted (bell) peppers, cut
into 2.5 cm/1 inch squares

1 red onion, finely diced

25 g/1 oz/1 cup fresh flat leaf
parsley, finely chopped

1 tsp salt

½ tsp black pepper

Crispy slices of chorizo, smoky piquillo peppers and nutty sherry vinegar make this a stellar salad. Piquillo peppers are special roasted peppers from Spain. They have a particular smoky flavour that is divine in salads. If you can't find them, simply substitute red roasted (bell) peppers.

Heat a non-stick pan until hot. Add the chorizo slices, in batches, and cook until crisp and brown. Drain on kitchen paper (paper towels).

Pour the dressing ingredients into a screw-top jar and shake well.

Combine the chickpeas (garbanzo), piquillo peppers, onion, parsley and chorizo in a medium bowl.

Just before serving, pour the dressing over the salad and mix gently.

GET ORGANIZED

The dressing can be made the day before and the salad ingredients can be assembled 6 hours before serving.

VARIATIONS

Merguez lamb sausages or Italian pepperoni could be used in place of chorizo. Harissa Dressing (see page 151) would complement the same ingredients. Spanish Manchego, goats cheese or feta cheese could be added.

saffron couscous

with roasted vegetables and harissa dressing

Aromatic saffron couscous topped with sweet roasted vegetables, a spicy harissa vinaigrette and cool refreshing yogurt dressing make a perfect one dish meal with a myriad of flavours. Try to use the fine grain couscous sold in Middle Eastern stores or on ethnic food internet sites. It's far more delicate than the supermarket variety.

SERVES 6 (APPETIZER), 4 (MAIN COURSE) OR AND 8 (SIDE DISH)

PREPARATION TIME: 50 MINUTES

1 tsp saffron threads, crushed

150 ml/¼ pint/ ⅔ cup vegetable or chicken stock

250 g/8 oz/1⅓ cups couscous

700 g/1½ lb sweet potatoes, peeled and cut into 1 cm/ ½ inch chunks

4 red onions, cut into large chunks

3 red (bell) peppers, de-seeded and cut into large pieces

4 tbsp olive oil

2 tbsp balsamic vinegar

1 tsp each salt and black pepper

1 quantity Harissa Dressing (see page 151)

handful of chopped fresh mint and coriander (cilantro)

FOR THE YOGURT SAUCE

2 tbsp extra virgin olive oil

juice of 1 lemon

200 ml/7 fl oz/scant 1 cup Greek (plain, strained) yogurt

1/2 tsp salt and black pepper

20 g/¾ oz/¾ cup fresh mint, chopped

Combine the saffron with stock. Pour it over the couscous, mix well and set aside for 30 minutes.

Heat oven to 200°C/400°F/Gas Mark 6. Arrange the sweet potatoes, onions and (bell) peppers in a roasting pan and drizzle with the oil, vinegar and salt and pepper. Roast for 40 minutes.

Combine the harissa dressing ingredients in a screw-top jar, shake well to mix and set aside.

For the yogurt sauce: Combine all the ingredients in a small bowl, stir to mix well, then chill in the refrigerator until required.

Break up the couscous with your fingers, making sure that there are no lumps, then tip it on to a large serving platter or into a large bowl. Place the roasted vegetables on top and pour the harissa dressing over them. Sprinkle chopped mint and coriander (cilantro) over the salad and serve with the yogurt sauce on the side.

GETTING ORGANIZED

The dressing and yogurt sauce can be prepared the day before, but add the fresh herbs just before serving. The vegetables could be roasted 4 hours ahead, but may look less attractive than if done only 1-2 hours before.

VARIATIONS

Pan-fried halloumi cheese, crumbled feta or shredded chicken could be included.

puy lentils with crispy salami, dill and mustard vinaigrette

The idea for tossing lentils with crispy salami and a zesty herb mustard dressing came from Divertimenti Café, one of the places where I teach classes. When it comes to lentils, Puy are the aristocrats. Unlike other varieties, which tend to disintegrate, Puy hold their shape magnificently and are coloured a stunning charcoal-green colour.

Place the lentils in a pan with salt, add cold water to cover and bring to the boil. Boil for 7–10 minutes or until al dente. Drain and place in a medium bowl.

Cook the pepperoni, chorizo or other salami in a large sauté pan until crisp, then drain on Kitchen paper (paper towels).

Add the salami, celery, tomatoes, onion, olives, dill, parsley and pepper to the lentils. Combine the mustard vinaigrette ingredients in a screw-top jar and shake well. Pour the dressing over the lentils and mix well. Season with additional salt and pepper if necessary.

SERVES 6 (APPETIZER), 4 (MAIN COURSE) OR 8 (SIDE DISH)

PREPARATION TIME: 30 MINUTES

250 g/8 oz/1 cup Puy lentils, rinsed

1 tsp salt

200 g/7 oz pepperoni, chorizo or other stick salami, sliced and halved

1 celery heart, finely chopped

250 g/8 oz cherry tomatoes, halved

1 small red onion, finely chopped

100 g/3½ oz/scant ½ cup pitted black olives, sliced

15 g/½ oz/½ cup fresh dill, finely chopped

15 g/½ oz/½ cup fresh flat leaf parsley, finely chopped

½ tsp black pepper

1 quantity Grainy Mustard Vinaigrette (see page 151)

GET ORGANIZED

The entire salad can be prepared the night before, but don't add the onion and ½ the dressing quantity until just before serving.

VARIATIONS

Different cheeses, such as feta, Gorgonzola or goat's cheese, could be added. Crispy slices of Italian pork and fennel sausage, can replace the salami. Slices of poached chicken breast or lamb would also be lovely.

borlotti beans
with tuna, celery and lemon dressing

I love to make this for a quick lunch as most of the ingredients are usually in my cupboard (pantry) or refrigerator. If you have never had Italian or Spanish tuna packed in olive oil, you are in for a great surprise. Although not inexpensive, it is miles beyond the banal supermarket variety. The rich silky tuna is a perfect partner for the creamy borlotti beans and tart lemon dressing.

Combine the beans, celery, onion, salt, pepper and parsley in a medium bowl.

Pour all the dressing ingredients into a screw-top jar and shake to combine. Mix the beans with the dressing and then transfer to a shallow serving dish. Arrange the tuna and eggs on top and serve.

SERVES 6 (APPETIZER), 4 (MAIN COURSE) OR 8 (SIDE DISH)

PREPARATION TIME: 10 MINUTES

2 x 400 g/14 oz cans borlotti beans, drained and rinsed, or 250 g/8 oz/1¼ cups dried borlotti beans, soaked overnight and boiled for 1-2 hours or until tender

2 celery hearts with leaves, thinly sliced

1 red onion, finely chopped

½ tsp each salt and black pepper

1 large handful of fresh parsley, finely chopped

1 quantity Lemon and Olive Oil Dressing (see page 152)

250 g/8 oz can Italian or Spanish tuna in olive oil, drained

2 hard-boiled (hard-cooked) eggs, quartered

GET ORGANIZED

The dressing and eggs can be made the day before. The salad can be prepared about 4 hours before serving and stored in the refrigerator. It may be wise to keep the onion separate so that it doesn't overpower the other flavours.

VARIATIONS

Fresh white crab meat or prawns (shrimp) could replace the tuna. Add radicchio lettuce, blanched green beans or sliced potatoes. Anchovy, Caper and Garlic Dressing (see page 150) or Classic Red Wine Vinaigrette (see page 150) could be used in place of the lemon.

tabbouleh with preserved lemon

SERVES 6 (APPETIZER),
4 (MAIN COURSE) OR
8 (SIDE DISH)

PREPARATION TIME:
1 HOUR

100 g/3½ oz/generous ½ cup
fine bulgar wheat

juice of 2 lemons

125 ml/4 fl oz/½ cup extra
virgin olive oil

1 large red onion, finely diced

1 tsp ground cumin

½ tsp ground cinnamon

1 tsp salt

3 small Lebanese cucumbers,
finely diced, or 1 medium
cucumber, de-seeded and
finely diced

4 plum tomatoes, de-seeded
and finely diced

2 large bunches of fresh flat
leaf parsley, finely chopped

1 large bunch of fresh mint
leaves, finely chopped

6 spring onions (scallions),
thinly sliced

1 preserved lemon, rind only,
rinsed and chopped

This ubiquitous Middle Eastern mezze salad has its origins in Lebanon. Don't be alarmed at the quantity of parsley called for here; the ratio of the herb to wheat is traditional. Although any cucumber could be used, Lebanese cucumbers are preferred for their intense aroma and crunchy texture, and are far less watery than their unexceptional hothouse cousins. They are easily found in Middle Eastern stores. Preserved lemons are lemons pickled in salt and sugar. They add an intense lemon flavour that is unique to them.

Rinse the bulgar wheat in several changes of cold water, pouring it back and forth between a large bowl and a very fine strainer, until the water runs clear. Drain again, place in a bowl and cover with the lemon juice and olive oil and leave to soak for 30 minutes

Meanwhile, combine the remaining ingredients in a large bowl. Add the lemon-soaked bulgar wheat, toss well, taste, and add more lemon or salt if necessary.

GET ORGANIZED

This salad will keep for 48 hours in the refrigerator, but is best eaten within 24 hours.

VARIATIONS

Add slices of grilled chicken breast for a substantial main course. Replace the parsley with watercress for a spicy taste. Chopped dried apricots and feta cheese could replace the preserved lemon for sweet and salty flavours.

rosemary cannellini beans

with parmesan and roasted cherry tomatoes

SERVES 6 (APPETIZER),
4 (MAIN COURSE) OR
8 (SIDE DISH)

PREPARATION TIME:
20 MINUTES

**250 g/8 oz cherry
tomatoes, halved**

6 tbsp olive oil

3 garlic cloves, chopped

**1 large red onion,
finely chopped**

2 tsp chopped fresh rosemary

**2 x 400 g/14 oz cans
cannellini beans, drained and
rinsed, or 250 g/8 oz/1¼ cups
dried cannellini beans, soaked
overnight and boiled for
1-2 hours or until tender**

**1 medium red onion,
finely chopped**

**60 g/2 oz/⅔ cup coarsely
grated or shaved
Parmesan cheese**

5 tbsp balsamic vinegar

**1 tsp each salt and freshly
ground black pepper**

A creamy yet firm texture is what distinguishes cannellini beans from other pulses. They are remarkably good from a can and even more luscious if you soak dried beans and boil them yourself. A *soffrito* of garlic, onion and rosemary is the secret to this salad's depth of flavour. The roasted tomatoes, crunchy red onion and Parmesan make it even more memorable.

Heat the oven to 200°C/400°F/Gas Mark 6.

Place the cherry tomato halves, cut side up, on a baking (cookie) sheet, drizzle with 4 tbsp of the olive oil and roast for 15 minutes. Remove them from the sheet and set aside.

Heat the remaining olive oil, the garlic, large red onion and rosemary over a low heat for about 4 minutes until soft. Add the beans and vinegar and cook until the beans are heated through.

Add the medium red onion, Parmesan, salt and pepper. Toss together and place the roasted cherry tomatoes on top.

GET ORGANIZED

The entire salad can be prepared 6 hours ahead, but don't add onion until just before serving.

VARIATIONS

Olive oil packed tuna (try to use imported Italian or Spanish) or blanched green beans could be added. Use as a base for grilled meats such as lamb or chicken.

you say tomato...

The French name for tomatoes, *pommes d'amour* – love apples – so aptly describes this prized vegetable. It's pure inspiration just to look at their ruby red lustre and smell their earthy scent. If one had to choose a desert island vegetable, it would have to be the tomato. No other

food can compare with its juiciness and burst of freshness. There are innumerable shapes, colours and sizes. From the regal beefsteak to the tasty sweet cherry tomato, the possibilities are endless.

tomato intelligence

There are very few countries, with the exception of those in Asia, that do not embrace tomatoes. Originally from Peru, they were brought to the rest of the world by the Spanish conquistadors. Technically they are fruits, but are used in salads and cooking as a vegetable. Their intense colour is from lycopene, which is also a powerful anti-oxidant. They also contain high levels of vitamins A, C and E. Some of these nutrients can be lost during cooking, so eating tomatoes raw in salads provides the highest concentration of nutrients.

Most tomatoes are sold under-ripe, so give them a couple of days to finish maturing. Their favourite home is a wire or wicker basket that allows air to circulate. Refrigeration changes the texture of the flesh and prevents them from ripening further.

There are hundreds of innocuous names for tomato varieties, which can change from regions or countries. Stay clear of names such as Moneymaker, Red Ponderosa or Mortgage Lifter; although commercially successful, these varieties are not renowned for their flavour. When choosing tomatoes for salads, think about what kind of taste, texture, and colour you're looking for. Each group is based on shape and size; with texture, water and seed content and flavour unique to each.

BEEFSTEAK (1)

The largest of all the tomatoes, beefsteak, beef or heirloom have a dense texture, few seeds and excellent flavour. They must be left to ripen before using or little taste will exist. Sold either green or bright red, they are ideal for sliced tomato salads. The green specimens will eventually turn red if they are left to ripen for long enough. Because of their sturdy texture, they are particularly good pan-fried with polenta or cornmeal. The best variety to look for is the Marmande, which has a bumpy and irregular shape and is sourced from Provence or Sicily. Delice (French) or Momotara (British) are also good choices with juicy flesh and sweet taste.

PLUM (2)

Oval or pear-shaped, these tomatoes range from small to medium. They are sometimes called Roma, as they are predominately grown and exported from southern Italy. The San Marzano variety is particularly elongated in shape and mostly used for high-quality canned tomatoes. Prized for their meaty flesh, sweet taste and low water content, they are perfect for chopping or roasting in salads. Both yellow and red varieties are produced, but the latter is more dependable for flavour. The tiny egg-shaped plum tomatoes are called pomodorino (Italian or Spanish), Santa (British), Midi (British) or Grape (American). Gorgeously sweet and available most of the year, they are invaluable in winter when the tomato selection is grim.

CHERRY (3)

These have the highest sugar content of all tomatoes, which explains why they taste so sweet. Despite their tough skins, they are juicy and delicious and work best left whole or simply halved. Red is the predominant colour, but they are also grown in yellow, gold and orange varieties, with names such as Sun-gold or Golden Delight. They are sold by weight or packaged as vine-ripened, still attached to the stem. In both cases, the quality can vary, so use your discretion. Not seen very often, the red and yellow teardrop tomatoes are particularly good for colour and taste. They are more likely to be found at farmers' markets than grocery stores.

ROUND (4)

The ubiquitous standard tomato seen in most stores is medium in size, full fleshed, but heavy with seeds and water. They are best for slicing or cut into quarters. Most are sold commercially and are extremely under-ripe. Give them two days minimum to gain some colour. Soil grown, organic or vine-ripened are the most notable and tasty. The yellow variety called Sunburst, has a bright lemon colour, but sadly not much flavour. Some popular red British varieties are the Regency, Rochelle (vine-ripened) or Gardener's Delight. Hydroponic or hothouse tomatoes are tasteless creations that should be avoided at all times unless desperate.

1

2

3

4

beefsteak tomatoes
with miso vinaigrette

SERVES 6 (APPETIZER),
4 (MAIN MEAL) OR
8 (SIDE DISH)

PREPARATION TIME:
10 MINUTES

4 large, firm ripe red or yellow beefsteak or other large meaty tomatoes, cut into 1 cm/½ inch slices

mizuna or rocket (arugula) leaves (optional)

4 spring onions (scallions), cut into fine batons

1 quantity Miso Ginger Dressing (see page 153)

1 tbsp sesame seeds

Miso, a fermented barley paste from Japan, has a nutty, salty taste that's scrumptious in dressings and superb spread on grilled aubergines (eggplant). It's also incredibly healthy – a great bonus. Look for it in Japanese, gourmet or health food stores.

Arrange the tomato slices and a small handful of mizuna or rocket (arugula) on a large platter.

Sprinkle the spring onions (scallions) over the top.

Combine the dressing ingredients in screw-top jar and shake well. Pour the dressing over the tomatoes and sprinkle with the sesame seeds. Serve immediately.

GET ORGANIZED

The dressing can be made in the morning and the salad prepared a couple of hours before serving. Keep the onions aside until just before serving.

VARIATIONS

Grilled aubergines (eggplant) are delicious with this dressing and could used in place of the tomatoes. Soy, Shallot and Ginger Dressing (see page 153) or Harissa Dressing (see page 151, omitting sesame seeds) could be used as well.

tomato, sourdough garlic croûton
and parmesan salad with balsamic dressing

SERVES 6 (APPETIZER),
4 (MAIN COURSE) OR
8 (SIDE DISH)

PREPARATION TIME:
30 MINUTES

500 g/1¼ lb ripe cherry tomatoes, halved, or 8 plum tomatoes, de-seeded and coarsely chopped

1 large red onion, diced

1 quantity sourdough Garlic Croûtons (see page 156)

100 g/3½ oz/generous 1 cup coarsely grated Parmesan

1 large bunch of fresh basil, coarsely chopped

1 quantity Balsamic Dressing (see page 152)

Ripe tomatoes are essential for this recipe. For the ultimate croûtons, use sourdough bread which retains its crunch even after soaking up the wonderful balsamic vinaigrette. Basil and Parmesan cheese make this a perfect summer salad.

Mix together the tomatoes, onion, croûtons, Parmesan and fresh basil in large bowl.

Just before serving, pour the dressing over the salad and mix again.

GET ORGANIZED

The croûtons can be made 2 days in advance and stored in an airtight container. The dressing can be made the day before. The salad can be made in the morning, but keep the onion separate until serving.

VARIATIONS

Crispy pieces of prosciutto could be added and Gorgonzola cheese or feta substituted for Parmesan.

tomato, asparagus and gorgonzola salad

In spring, nothing beats tender spears of asparagus blanched to perfection. Here, they're made even more irresistible by adding Gorgonzola cheese and diced tomatoes. If you can't find worthy standard tomatoes, try using quartered cherry ones.

SERVES 6 (APPETIZER), 4 (MAIN COURSE) OR 8 (SIDE DISH)

PREPARATION TIME: 20 MINUTES

500 g/1¼ lb thin asparagus spears, trimmed

juice of ½ lemon

4 tbsp extra virgin olive oil

1 tsp salt

6 plum or vine ripened tomatoes, de-seeded and diced

1 garlic clove, finely chopped

2 shallots, finely chopped

1 large bunch of fresh basil, finely shredded

½ tsp freshly ground black pepper

100 g/3½ oz Gorgonzola or Roquefort cheese, crumbled

Bring a large pan of salted water to the boil. Drop in the asparagus and blanch for 1 minute. Drain and immediately immerse in iced water to prevent any further cooking (this leaves the asparagus bright green).

Make a lemon vinaigrette by mixing together the lemon juice, olive oil and half the salt in a screw-top jar and shaking well.

Place the tomatoes in medium bowl and add the lemon vinaigrette, garlic, shallots, basil, the remaining salt and pepper to taste. Set aside.

Arrange the asparagus on a large platter or individual serving plates. Pour the tomato mixture over it and place the crumbled cheese on top to serve.

GET ORGANIZED

The dressing can be prepared the day before. The asparagus and tomato mixture can be made 6 hours in advance, but add the fresh basil and the dressing just before serving.

VARIATIONS

Place toasted bread under the asparagus to soak up the lovely dressing. Tiny capers or black olives could be added to the tomato mixture. Other cheeses, such as goats cheese, mozarella or feta, could relace the Gorgonzola.

Greek salad

Surely the Greeks never intended their salad to be so misunderstood. If you've ever visited Greece, you must wonder where it all went sadly wrong. As we don't have access to the same sun-kissed vegetables that they do, an anchovy caper dressing makes the cucumbers, creamy feta and tomatoes taste not far off the real thing. Great with leg of lamb or a summer barbecue.

Place the tomatoes, onion and cucumbers in large bowl.

Combine all the dressing ingredients in screw-top jar and shake well.

Just before serving, add the feta to the bowl of vegetables. Pour the dressing over the salad and sprinkle with oregano. Season with salt and pepper, if necessary.

SERVES 6 (APPETIZER), 4 (MAIN COURSE) OR 8 (SIDE DISH)

PREPARATION TIME: 15 MINUTES

500g/1¼ lb cherry tomatoes, halved, or 6 vine-ripened tomatoes, coarsely chopped

1 large red onion, diced

4 small Lebanese cucumbers, sliced, or 1 large cucumber, de-seeded and sliced

1 quantity Anchovy, Caper and Garlic Dressing (see page 150)

200 g/7 oz feta cheese, drained and cut into 2.5 cm/ 1 inch cubes

1 tbsp chopped fresh oregano or 1 tsp dried oregano

salt and freshly ground black pepper (optional)

GET ORGANIZED

The vegetables and dressing can be assembled the morning. Slice the cheese shortly before serving.

VARIATIONS

Diced cooked lamb or chicken would be a good addition. Whole caper berries, grilled halloumi cheese, chopped dill and mint could be added as well.

tomato and iceberg lettuce wedges
with catalina dressing

When I was a girl, I begged my mother to buy a bottled dressing I thought exotic for its bright orange colour and mysterious name, Catalina. She refused, horrified by the artificial ingredients, but said we could create our own version. What resulted was a tangy dressing made from cider vinegar, olive oil and, believe or not, ketchup. It is particularly good on crunchy iceberg lettuce and ripe tomatoes. The iceberg must be dense for maximum crunch, so look for heavy heads of lettuce.

Place the lettuce wedges on plates and arrange the tomato wedges and spring onions (scallions) on each one.

For the dressing: Whisk together the vinegar, sugar, salt, pepper, ketchup, water, Worcestershire sauce, lemon juice, olive oil and coriander seeds in a small bowl. Set aside until required.

Just before serving, pour the dressing over the salad and sprinkle with the chives.

SERVES 6 (APPETIZER) OR 8 (SIDE DISH)

PREPARATION TIME: 10 MINUTES

1 iceberg lettuce, cored and cut into 4 pieces

4 vine-ripened tomatoes, cut into wedges

4 spring onions (scallions), cut into 2.5 cm/1 inch pieces

25 g/1 oz/¼ cup finely chopped fresh chives

FOR THE DRESSING

75 ml/2 fl oz/¼ cup cider vinegar

1½ tsp sugar

2 tsp sea salt

1 tsp black pepper

125 ml/4 fl oz/½ cup tomato ketchup, preferably organic

3 tbsp water

11/2 tsp Worcestershire sauce

11/2 tbsp fresh lemon juice

125 ml/4 fl oz/½ cup olive oil

1 tsp coriander seeds, coarsely crushed or cracked

GET ORGANIZED

The dressing will keep for 3 days and the salad plates can be prepared in the morning.

VARIATIONS

Crumbled Roquefort cheese, Prosciutto Bits (see page 157) or Garlic Croûtons (see page 156) can be sprinkled over the salad with the chives. The lettuce can be sliced into bite-sized pieces instead of quartered.

green bean, tomato and mozzarella salad
with anchovy, caper and garlic dressing

Creamy buffalo mozzarella, sweet tomatoes and crunchy green beans are drizzled with a piquant dressing. The dressing is very moreish, so keep your crust of bread to mop up the very last drops. Budget allowing, try to buy buffalo mozzarella because it does make a difference.

SERVES 6 (APPETIZER),
4 (MAIN COURSE) OR
10 (SIDE DISH)

PREPARATION TIME:
20 MINUTES

300 g/11 oz/2 cups fine green beans, trimmed

300g/11 oz mixed yellow and red cherry tomatoes, halved

1 onion, halved and thinly sliced

250 g/8 oz bocconcini (mini mozzarella) or 2 buffalo mozzarella balls, cut into 2 cm/1 inch pieces and drained on kitchen paper (paper towels)

3 tbsp shredded fresh basil

1 quantity Anchovy, Caper and Garlic Dressing (see page 150)

fresh basil leaves, to garnish

Cook the beans in a large pan of salted, boiling water until al dente. Drain and immediately immerse in iced water for 5 minutes or until chilled. Drain on kitchen paper (paper towels).

This salad looks most beautiful composed rather than tossed, so place the ingredients on a large platter, arranging the beans, tomatoes, onion and mozzarella in separate piles.

Sprinkle shredded basil over the top and drizzle with the dressing just before serving. Garnish with whole basil leaves.

GET ORGANIZED

Blanch the green beans and make the dressing up to 24 hours ahead. Slice the tomatoes up to 2 hours ahead. The basil, mozzarella, and onion can be prepared up to 1 hour ahead. Assemble the salad shortly before serving.

VARIATIONS

Pan-fried halloumi cheese could be used instead of mozzarella. Slices of barbecue-cooked lamb or chicken would make a substantial addition. Balsamic Dressing (see page 152) could be used.

Tunisian spicy roast pepper
and tomato salad

This is a classic North African salad known as Meshwiya. Although the list of ingredients might seem bizarre, make no mistake – this is a serious salad. A perfect addition to a mezze selection.

**SERVES 6 (APPETIZER),
4 (MAIN COURSE) OR
8 (SIDE DISH)**

**PREPARATION TIME:
30 MINUTES**

**3 red (bell) peppers,
de-seeded and quartered**

5 plum tomatoes

**½ tsp each salt and
black pepper**

**2 garlic cloves, finely
crushed (minced)**

1 tsp cumin seeds

**1 tsp harissa or other chilli
paste (optional)**

**½ tsp sweet paprika
(pimenton preferably)**

juice of ½ lemon

3 tbsp extra virgin olive oil

**20g/½ oz/½ cup fresh flat leaf
parsley, finely chopped**

**4 hard-boiled (hard-cooked)
quail's eggs, halved, or
2 hard-boiled hen's eggs,
cut into wedges**

8 pitted black olives

**½ preserved lemon, rind
only, rinsed and chopped
(optional)**

Heat the grill (broiler).

Place the (bell) peppers, skin side up, on a baking (cookie) sheet and grill (broil), turning frequently, until blackened all over. Transfer to a plastic bag, seal and set aside for 10 minutes. Peel off the skins and slice each quarter in half.

Cut the tomatoes into halves. Arrange the tomatoes, cut side up, on a baking (cookie) sheet. Season with salt and pepper and grill (broil) for 5 minutes or until blackened.

Place the tomatoes, red peppers, garlic, cumin, harissa, paprika, lemon juice, olive oil and parsley in a bowl. Toss gently and add salt and pepper to taste.

Tip the salad onto a large platter and arrange the eggs on top. Sprinkle the olives and preserved lemon rind over the salad.

GET ORGANIZED

The entire salad can be made 4 hours ahead and stored in the refrigerator.

VARIATIONS

You can omit the eggs and use the remaining salad as a topping for bread. Seared tuna or swordfish would be lovely with this. Capers are a tasty addition.

polenta-fried beefsteak tomatoes with corn,
lime and coriander (cilantro) vinaigrette

Tomatoes are fried with a crispy coating and then drizzled with a zesty corn vinaigrette with lime and coriander. Although sometimes difficult to find, green tomatoes would be outstanding in place of red beefsteaks.

SERVES 6 (APPETIZER), 4 (MAIN COURSE) OR 8 (SIDE DISH)

PREPARATION TIME: 25 MINUTES

2 corn cobs or 100 g/ 3½ oz/generous ½ cup thawed frozen or drained canned corn kernels

5 tbsp olive oil

juice of 2 limes

1 chipotle in adobo or small green chilli, de-seeded and finely chopped

1 tbsp extra virgin olive oil

1 small handful of fresh coriander (cilantro), finely chopped

pinch of cayenne pepper

1 tsp each salt and black pepper

4 ripe beefsteak, green or other large ripe tomatoes

150 g/5 oz/1 cup polenta or cornmeal

4 small handfuls of rocket (arugula)

If using fresh corn cobs, cut off the kernels. Heat 1 tbsp of the olive oil in a pan, add the corn kernels and cook 5 minutes or until tender. Remove from pan with a slotted soon and place in small bowl.

Add the lime juice, chilli, extra virgin olive oil, coriander (cilantro), cayenne and half the salt and pepper.

Cut the tomatoes into 1 cm/½ inch thick slices. Use only the 3–4 large slices from the middle of each tomato.

Heat the remaining olive oil in a pan. Meanwhile, dredge the tomato slices in polenta or cornmeal to coat, then season with the remaining salt and pepper. Cook until crispy, then remove from the pan and drain on kitchen paper (paper towels).

Place the rocket (arugula) on individual plates or a large platter. Arrange the tomatoes on top and spoon the corn vinaigrette over them. Serve immediately.

GET ORGANIZED

The tomatoes can be fried 1 hour before eating and vinaigrette can be made in the morning.

VARIATIONS

Slices of mozzarella would lovely with the tomatoes. You can substitute Citrus Caper Dressing (see page 150) for the vinaigrette. Pan-fried thinly pounded chicken breasts would be fantastic served under the tomatoes.

panzanella salad

This is a to-die-for tomato salad from Tuscany laced with roasted (bell) peppers, olives, crunchy cucumber, capers and chewy bread. It's perfect in hot weather and my idea of dream food.

SERVES 6 (APPETIZER),
4 (MAIN COURSE) OR
8 (SIDE DISH)

PREPARATION TIME:
20 MINUTES

1 ciabatta or sourdough loaf, cut into 1 cm/½ inch cubes

2 red (bell) peppers, de-seeded and cut into quarters

500 g/1¼ lb cherry tomatoes, halved, or 6 plum tomatoes, de-seeded and chopped into 1 cm/½ inch pieces

3 celery sticks, sliced

10 Italian black olives, pitted and halved

2 tbsp capers, rinsed

1 red onion, finely chopped

2–3 mini cucumbers, peeled and sliced, or 1 standard cucumber, peeled, de-seeded and sliced

20 fresh basil leaves, shredded

1 small bunch of fresh flat leaf parsley, chopped

1 anchovy, rinsed and chopped

1 garlic clove, finely chopped

4 tbsp extra virgin olive oil

4 tbsp good quality red wine vinegar

1 tsp salt

1 tsp freshly ground black pepper

Heat the oven to 200°C/400°F/Gas Mark 6 and heat the grill (broiler).

Spread out the bread cubes on a baking (cookie) sheet and toast in the oven for 5 minutes or until the croûtons are crisp. Remove from the oven and set aside.

Place the red (bell) peppers on large baking sheet, skin side up. Grill (broil) until blackened, then place in a plastic bag, seal and set aside for 5 minutes. Remove from bag and peel off the skins. Thinly slice the flesh and place in large bowl.

Add the tomatoes, celery, olives, capers, onion, cucumbers, basil, parsley, anchovy and garlic and mix well.

When ready to serve, drizzle the oil and vinegar over the salad, season with salt and pepper and serve.

GET ORGANIZED

The salad ingredients can be assembled the day before, keeping the garlic, onion, anchovy, basil, and oil and vinegar separate. Mix together just before serving.

VARIATIONS

Slices of grilled chicken would be a substantial and tasty addition. Chunks of mozzarella, Parmesan or other Italian cheese would be delicious.

leaves, greens and other things

Nothing is more refreshing than a bowl of delicate, crisp lettuces, tossed with vinegar and olive oil. You could leave it at that and want nothing more than a piece of bread to mop up the remaining dressing. The varieties are remarkable — from the spicy leaves of mizuna to the sweet green and pink-speckled red oak leaf. Create a crunchy base for other vegetables and cheeses or — best of all — keep it simple.

chicory (Belgian endive), watercress and pear salad with blue cheese and sherry vinegar and walnut oil vinaigrette

These ingredients are made for each other. The bitter chicory (Belgian endive) is mellowed by sweet pear, salty cheese and spicy watercress. It's all pulled together with crispy pancetta and a nutty dressing – a luscious winter treat.

SERVES 6 (APPETIZER), 4 (MAIN COURSE) OR 8 (SIDE DISH)

PREPARATION TIME: 15 MINUTES

3 heads of chicory (Belgian endive), trimmed

1 large bunch of watercress, stems removed

large handful of frisée, inner white part only

2 pears, peeled, cored and chopped into 1 cm/ ½ inch pieces

juice of ½ lemon

250 g/8 oz pancetta, finely diced, or streaky (fatty) bacon rashers (strips)

100 g/3½ oz Roquefort, Gorgonzola or other piquant blue cheese

FOR THE DRESSING

3 tbsp sherry vinegar

4 tbsp walnut or hazelnut oil

2 tbsp extra virgin olive oil

½ tsp Dijon mustard

1 tsp sugar

½ tsp salt

½ tsp freshly ground black pepper

Slice the chicory (Belgian endive) into 2.5 cm/1 inch pieces and place in large serving bowl with the watercress and frisée.

Toss the pears with the lemon juice in a small bowl and set aside.

Fry the diced pancetta or bacon rashers (strips) until very crisp. Set the pancetta aside. Drain the bacon well on kitchen paper (paper towels) and then crumble.

Break the cheese into small pieces or freeze it for 10 minutes and then grate.

Mix all the dressing ingredients in a screw-top jar and shake well.

Just before serving, add the pears, pancetta or bacon, cheese and dressing to the salad bowl and toss well.

GET ORGANIZED

The salad should be made no more than 2 hours before eating. The dressing can be made the day before.

VARIATIONS

The dressing can be added to the hot pan after cooking the pancetta or bacon and served warm over the salad. Other bitter salad leaves, such as treviso (red chicory), could be used as well. Garlic Croûtons (see page 156) would be a tasty addition.

cos (romaine) hearts

with roquefort dressing

SERVES 6 (APPETIZER),
4 (MAIN COURSE) OR
8 (SIDE DISH)

PREPARATION TIME:
10 MINUTES

2 large Cos (romaine) hearts

1 small red onion, cut into thin rings

4 yellow or red vine-ripened tomatoes, cut into quarters (if using cherry tomatoes, leave whole)

FOR THE DRESSING

125 g/4 oz Roquefort or other piquant blue cheese, broken into chunks

1½ tbsp red wine or sherry vinegar

1 tsp black pepper

6 tbsp crème fraîche or sour cream

3 tbsp olive or vegetable oil

One of my favourite childhood meals was cooked by my father – steak, baked potatoes heaped with sour cream and iceberg lettuce with Roquefort dressing. Pure comfort food! With its rich texture and pungent salty flavour, blue veined Roquefort is one of the world's best cheeses.

For the dressing. Place all the dressing ingredients in a food processor and pulse until the mixture is creamy, then scrap into a bowl. Alternatively, mix all the ingredients together by hand.

Arrange whole lettuce leaves on a large platter. Place red onion rings and tomatoes on top and pour the dressing over the salad just before serving.

GET ORGANIZED

The dressing can made 3 days ahead and the salad 4 hours in advance. Do not add the onion until just before serving.

VARIATIONS

Garlic Croûtons (see page 156) or Proscuitto Bits (see page 157) would suit this nicely. Other sturdy lettuces such as iceberg could be used.

fattoush

1 Cos (romaine) lettuce, cut into 1 cm/½ inch ribbons

250 g/8 oz cherry tomatoes, halved

4 spring onions (scallions), thinly sliced

1 large cucumber, de-seeded and sliced, or 4 Lebanese mini cucumbers, sliced

15 radishes, thinly sliced

1 red (bell) pepper, de-seeded and cut into 1 cm/½ inch dice

small handful of fresh flat leaf parsley leaves

15 fresh mint leaves

1 quantity Pitta Croûtons (see page 156)

1 quantity Pomegranate Dressing (see page 150) or Lemon and Olive Oil Dressing (see page 152)

1 tbsp ground sumac (optional)

Although every Middle Eastern country claims its own version, the Lebanese are the originators of this salad. Crispy pieces of pitta bread are tossed with crunchy vegetables and a tart lemon and pomegranate dressing. The salad is sprinkled with a purple spice called sumac, a ground berry similar in appearance to a currant. It is available from spice shops or Middle eastern stores but if you can't find it, the salad is equally delicious without.

Combine the lettuce, tomatoes, spring onions (scallions), cucumber, radishes, (bell) pepper, parsley, mint and croûtons in a large bowl.

Pour all the dressing ingredients into a screw-top jar and shake well.

Just before serving, pour the dressing over the salad and sprinkle with the sumac, if using.

GET ORGANIZED

The dressing and salad can be made in the morning and the croûtons can be prepared 1 day ahead and stored in an airtight container.

VARIATIONS

Feta cheese and olives would be tasty additions. Any leftover shredded chicken or lamb would work as well. A handful of chopped fresh dill could be added.

chopped salad
with roasted garlic and herb dressing

Glorious ingredients – all made miniature. Soaking the radicchio in iced water removes the bitterness and gives it a beautiful, bright colour. Provolone, a mild smoky cheese shaped like a pear, can be found in Italian delicatessens and supermarkets. Alternatively, substitute another hard Italian cheese, such as asiago or pecorino (romano).

Soak the radicchio in iced water for 30 minutes to remove the bitterness.

Meanwhile, heat the oven to 200°C/400°F/Gas Mark 6.

Spread out the bread cubes on a baking (cookie) sheet and toast in the oven for 5 minutes until lightly browned. Remove from the oven and set aside.

Drain the radicchio and dry in salad spinner or pat dry with kitchen paper (paper towels). Place it in a large bowl with the chickpeas (garbanzo beans), onion, tomatoes, celery, palm hearts, pickled peppers, Parmesan, provolone and salami. Gently mix together.

Put all the dressing ingredients into a screw-top jar, shake well and pour over the salad just before serving. Sprinkle with chopped basil.

SERVES 6 (APPETIZER), 4 (MAIN COURSE) OR 8 (SIDE DISH)

PREPARATION TIME: 30 MINUTES

½ head of radicchio, thinly sliced

80 g/3 oz French or sourdough bread, cut into 1 cm/½ inch cubes

400 g/14 oz can chickpeas (garbanzo beans), drained and rinsed

1 red onion, finely chopped

100 g/3½ oz cherry tomatoes, halved

2 celery sticks from inner heart, finely chopped

400 g/14 oz can palm hearts, cut into large dice

10 pickled sweet cherry peppers (peppadew or peperoncini), finely chopped

60 g/2 oz/⅔ cup coarsely grated Parmesan cheese

60 g/2 oz provolone cheese, finely diced

100 g/3½ oz sliced pepperoni, napoli piccante or other Italian salami, coarsely chopped

1 quantity Roasted Garlic and Herb Dressing (see page 153)

1 small bunch of fresh basil, finely chopped

GET ORGANIZED

The salad can be prepared in the morning, but leave the onion, provolone, Parmesan and croûtons in separate containers. The dressing can be prepared the day before.

VARIATIONS

Chopped roasted (bell) peppers or chicken breast could be added as well. Peppadew (pickled cherry peppers) can be found in supermarkets and can be substituted with Italian or Turkish pickled peppers.

frisée and radicchio salad
with chopped egg, bacon and red wine vinaigrette

Chopped eggs are SO good with vinaigrette. Frisée, with its slender, yellow-white, curly leaves catches every drop of the dressing. Crispy bacon and colourful radicchio complete this satisfying, yet simple salad.

SERVES 6 (APPETIZER), 4 (MAIN COURSE) OR 8 (SIDE DISH)

PREPARATION TIME: 30 MINUTES

4 eggs (preferably organic)

1 large head of frisée, cored and dark green leaves removed

½ head of radicchio, cored and torn into 2.5 cm/1 inch pieces

400g/14 oz thin streaky (fatty) bacon rashers (strips) or pancetta, fried until very crisp

1½ quantity Classic Red Wine Vinaigrette (see page 150)

Bring a small pan of water to the boil. Lower the heat to a simmer, gently place the eggs in the water and cook for 12 minutes. Plunge the eggs into cold water to stop any further cooking. If you prefer your eggs soft-boiled, then boil for 3–5 minutes depending on their size.

Chop hard-boiled eggs into coarse dice. Slice soft-boiled eggs in half.

Arrange the frisée leaves on large platter and top with the radicchio. Place chopped hard-boiled eggs or soft-boiled egg halves on top.

You can either crumble the bacon or pancetta over the salad or leave in long strips on top.

Place all the vinaigrette ingredients in a screw-top jar and shake well. Pour the dressing over the salad and serve.

GET ORGANIZED

The dressing can be made the day before. The eggs can be prepared 2 days in advance and refrigerated. The salad leaves and bacon can be prepared in the morning.

VARIATIONS

The vinaigrette could be heated with the bacon or pancetta for a warm salad. Anchovy, Caper and Garlic Dressing (see page 150) would be delicious in place of the vinaigrette. Garlic Croûtons (see page 156), crumbled goat's cheese or roasted capers would work well.

classic caesar salad

To pay my way through university, I worked as a waitress in a formal restaurant that made Caesar salad at the tables. Perhaps it was a trend in the late 1970s. I still love this recipe, although now I mix the dressing in the food processor instead of whisking it in a large wooden bowl.

SERVES 6 (APPETIZER),
4 (MAIN COURSE) OR
8 (SIDE DISH)

PREPARATION TIME:
30 MINUTES

1 large Cos or romaine lettuce, torn into 2.5 cm/ 1 inch pieces, or 4 Little Gem (Bibb) lettuces, sliced into chunks

1 quantity Garlic Croûtons (see page 156), made without the garlic

2 large (extra large) egg yolks, at room temperature

2 anchovies, rinsed and chopped

2 tbsp Dijon mustard

1 large garlic clove, crushed

2 tsp Worcestershire sauce

1 tbsp red wine vinegar

175 ml/6 fl oz/¾ cup olive oil

juice of 1 lemon

60 g/2 oz/⅔ cup freshly grated Parmesan cheese

1 tsp freshly ground black pepper

salt (optional)

Place the lettuce and croûtons in a wooden bowl and set aside.

Put the egg yolks, anchovies, mustard and garlic in a food processor or blender and process until combined. Add the Worcestershire sauce and red wine vinegar. With motor running, gradually drizzle in the olive oil until the dressing is thick. Alternatively, whisk the egg yolks, anchovies, mustard and garlic in a bowl, then whisk in the Worcestershire sauce and vinegar until combined. Gradually whisk in the olive oil until thick and creamy.

Add the lemon juice and Parmesan and season with pepper. Taste and add salt or extra lemon juice, if necessary.

Scrape out of the bowl and toss with lettuce and croûtons just before serving.

GET ORGANIZED

The salad and dressing can be made in the morning, but do not combine until just before serving. The croûtons can be made 2 days in advance and stored in an airtight container.

VARIATIONS

Char-grilled slices of chicken, prawns (shrimp), crab, lobster and chunks of salmon are all delicious additions if the salad is eaten as a meal on its own. Try adding one of the accessories from the last chapter – Prosciutto Bits (see page 157), Oven-dried Tomatoes (see page 156) or Roasted Capers (see page 157).

puntarelle salad with anchovy dressing

Puntarelle is a bitter, green and white salad leaf related to the chicory (Belgian endive) and radicchio family. The Romans eat it in winter with a tangy lemon and anchovy dressing. They temper its bitterness by soaking it in iced water, which also imparts a crisp texture. Since Puntarelle is difficult to get obtain, you can use chicory instead. Treviso (red chicory) is particularly colourful.

If using puntarelle, split the hollow stalks lengthways into long strips. Cut the chicory, if using, into diagonal pieces. Soak them in iced water for 30 minutes. Drain and set aside.

Using a mortar and pestle, grind the anchovy filets and garlic to a paste, then transfer to small bowl. Whisk in the lemon juice or vinegar, olive oil and pepper.

Toss the salad with the dressing just before serving and grind fresh pepper over it.

SERVES 6 (APPETIZER), 4 (MAIN COURSE) OR 8 (SIDE DISH)

PREPARATION TIME: 30 MINUTES

2 heads of puntarelle, cored and trimmed of tough leaves or 4 heads of chicory (Belgian endive) or treviso (red chicory) dressing

5 Spanish or Italian anchovies packed in olive oil, rinsed

1 garlic clove

juice of 1 lemon or 1 tbsp white wine vinegar

3 tbsp extra virgin olive oil

freshly ground black pepper

GET ORGANIZED

The lettuce can be soaked in the morning and stored in the refrigerator. Make the dressing 1 hour before eating, but don't dress the salad until just before serving.

VARIATIONS

Crisp slices of radish or celery would add crunchy texture. Crab or seared prawns would make a tasty and substantial addition.

red oak leaf lettuce with crispy prosciutto,
gorgonzola and honey mustard dressing

Mild lettuces are tossed in sweet honey mustard dressing and then adorned with prosciutto and Gorgonzola for a delightful and quickly made salad.

Place the lettuces and radicchio leaves in a large bowl. Add (bell) pepper, celery, tomatoes and onions and set aside.

Prepare the prosciutto bits and toss them over salad.

Meanwhile put all the dressing ingredients into a screw-top jar and shake well.

Just before serving, pour the dressing over the salad. Crumble the cheese with your fingers and sprinkle it over the salad.

SERVES 6 (APPETIZER),
4 (MAIN COURSE) OR
8 (SIDE DISH)

PREPARATION TIME:
15 MINUTES

1 red oak leaf lettuce, torn
into 2.5 cm/1 inch pieces

½ round (butterhead) lettuce,
torn into 2.5 cm/1 inch

2–3 radicchio leaves, torn into
2.5 cm/1 inch pieces

1 red (bell) pepper, de-seeded
and cut into thin batons

2 small celery sticks (hearts
only), cut into thin slices

200 g/7 oz cherry
tomatoes, halved

2 small red onions, cut into
thin rings

1 quantity Prosciutto Bits
(see page 157)

125 g/4 oz Gorgonzola cheese

FOR THE DRESSING

5 tbsp light olive oil

1½ tbsp red wine vinegar

1 tbsp Dijon mustard

1 tbsp clear honey

½ garlic clove, finely chopped

½ tsp each salt and freshly
ground black pepper

GET ORGANIZED

The dressing can be made
24 hours ahead. The salad
can be assembled and in
the morning and stored
in the refrigerator, but do
not add the onions, cheese
and prosciutto until just
before serving.

VARIATIONS

Garlic Croûtons (see
page 156) or char-grilled
chicken would be a tasty
addition. For a less sweet
dressing you can substitute
Classic Red Wine Vinaigrette
(see page 150). Any type of
cheese, such as Roquefort,
Parmesan, feta or pecorino
(romano), could be used.

rocket (arugula), avocado and palm heart salad
with lemon and olive oil dressing

At Florence's Trattoria Garga, owned by an artist-husband and chef-wife, beautiful murals provide a stunning backdrop for unbelievable food. This is their house salad. It includes hearts of palm, a South American ingredient sold in cans at supermarkets.

Place the avocado in a bowl, add a squeeze of lemon juice to prevent discoloration and set aside.

Combine the rocket (arugula), radicchio, tomatoes, palm hearts, pine nuts and Parmesan in a bowl and season with salt and pepper.

Pour all the dressing ingredients into a screw-top jar and shake well.

Just before serving, add the avocado and pour the dressing over the salad. Mix well and serve immediately.

SERVES 6 (APPETIZER), 4 (MAIN COURSE) OR 8 (SIDE DISH)

PREPARATION TIME: 15 MINUTES

1 avocado, peeled, stoned (pitted) and coarsely diced

½ lemon

3 large bunches of rocket (arugula), trimmed

1 small head of radicchio, torn into small pieces

250 g/8 oz cherry tomatoes, halved

6 palm hearts, sliced into 1 cm/½ inch slices

100 g/3½ oz/scant 1 cup pine nuts toasted

100 g/3½ oz/generous 1 cup coarsely grated Parmesan cheese

salt and freshly ground black pepper

1 quantity Lemon and Olive Oil Dressing (see page 152)

GET ORGANIZED

The dressing can be made the day before. The salad can be prepared in the morning and refrigerated.

VARIATIONS

Grilled prawns (shrimp) or slices of grilled chicken would suit this salad well. Classic Red Wine Vinaigrette (see page 150) or Anchovy, Caper and Garlic Dressing (see page 150) could be substituted for the lemon dressing.

spinach salad
with warm prosciutto and champagne dressing

In the 1970s, spinach salad with hot bacon dressing was all the rage. This modern adaptation is lighter and healthier, but still impressive.

Heat the olive oil, prosciutto and garlic over a medium heat for about 3 minutes.

Add the wine, lemon juice, vinegar, sugar and salt and pepper. Simmer for about 5 minutes.

Remove from the heat and leave to cool slightly, then taste and add more lemon juice or sugar, if necessary.

Place the spinach on a large platter or in a big bowl. Sprinkle the mushrooms, red onions, walnuts and cheese over it.

Pour the dressing over the salad and mix just before serving.

SERVES 6 (APPETIZER), 4 (MAIN COURSE) OR 8 (SIDE DISH)

PREPARATION TIME: 20 MINUTES

6 tbsp extra virgin olive oil

12 slices prosciutto, finely diced

4 garlic cloves, finely chopped

6 tbsp dry white wine

6 tbsp fresh lemon juice

4 tbsp Champagne or white wine vinegar

4 tbsp sugar

½ tsp each salt and freshly ground black pepper

350 g/12 oz baby spinach

350 g/12 oz small mushrooms, sliced

2 small red onions, sliced into 1 cm/½ inch rings

125 g/4 oz/1 cup toasted chopped walnuts

80 g/3 oz/1 cup coarsely grated Parmesan cheese

GET ORGANIZED

The dressing can be made day before and stored in the refrigerator. The salad can be prepared in the morning, but don't slice or add the onions until the last minute.

VARIATIONS

You can add the mushrooms to the warm dressing to pour over the salad, instead of serving them raw. Alternative dressings, such as Classic Red Wine Vinaigrette (see page 150) or Sherry and Olive Oil Vinaigrette (see page 150) could be used.

antipasto salad

This type of salad, although popular in Italian-American restaurants, isn't found in Italy. But who says you have to be a slave to authenticity? I was inspired when I had this at Carmine's, a family style trattoria, in New York City. Artichoke hearts, pickled peppers, and crisp lettuce are tossed in a deliciously sweet red wine vinaigrette.

Put all the vinaigrette ingredients into a screw-top jar and shake well to mix.

Place all the remaining ingredients in a large bowl.

Just before serving, pour the dressing over the salad and toss well.

SERVES 6 (APPETIZER), 4 (MAIN COURSE) OR 8 (SIDE DISH)

PREPARATION TIME: 30 MINUTES

1 quantity Classic Red Wine Vinaigrette (see page 150)

2 hearts of Cos or romaine lettuce, torn into 2.5 cm/ 1 inch pieces

2 x 175g/6 oz jars marinated artichoke hearts, drained

handful of pitted black olives, sliced

1 red onion, thinly sliced into rings

1 red (bell) pepper, de-seeded and thinly sliced

250 g/8 oz cherry tomatoes, halved

1 large handful of peppadew (pepperoncini) or other sweet pickled peppers

60 g/2 oz Italian salami (pepperoni, napoli piccante or Milano), thinly sliced

GET ORGANIZED

The dressing can be prepared a day ahead and the salad 2 hours before, but no earlier or the artichokes will make the lettuce soggy.

VARIATIONS

Bocconcini (mini balls of mozzarella) could be added. Roasted peppers could replace the raw peppers. Sliced hearts of palm could replace the artichokes.

bring on the vegetables

5

Each season launches a cornucopia of new vegetables; spring arrives with green-purple hued baby artichokes, summer introduces ripe tomatoes, autumn (fall) follows with neon orange squash, and winter ushers in earthy beetroot (beets) and sweet potatoes. Follow the growing periods and you will be rewarded with sweet vegetables that taste just like you imagine. Greenhouse impostors should be ignored if at all possible.

roasted baby beetroot (beets)
with warm goat's cheese cakes in breadcrumbs

**8 baby beetroot (beets) or
4 medium size beetroot,
well scrubbed**

2 tbsp olive oil

1½ tsp sea salt

**1 tsp freshly ground
black pepper**

4 hard goat's cheese crottins

**125 g/4 oz/2 cups sourdough
or other high-quality
breadcrumbs**

1 egg, beaten

**1 quantity Balsamic Dressing
(see page 152)**

4 handfuls of rocket (arugula)

Bad childhood memories of canned beetroot (beets) still haunt many adults. My husband, a sworn beetroot hater, was finally converted when I made this dish. To produce a sweet, earthy flavour, select small beetroot and roast them. Add crispy goat's cheese cakes and a sweet balsamic dressing – you might find yourself swooning!

Heat the oven to 200°C/400°F/Gas Mark 6.

Place whole baby beetroot (beets) on a large piece of foil. Cut larger ones in half or quarters and place on a sheet of foil. Drizzle with olive oil and season 1 tsp salt and ½ tsp pepper. Wrap into a parcel and roast for 30-40 minutes until the beetroot is tender and easily pierced with the point of a knife.

Slice the crottins in half and mould into a round. Add the remaining salt and pepper to the breadcrumbs. Dip the cheese rounds into the beaten egg, then roll in the breadcrumbs to coat. Chill in the refrigerator for at least 20 minutes.

Put all the dressing ingredients in a screw-top jar, shake well and set aside.

When the beetroot is cooked, slice baby ones in half or peel and thickly slice larger ones. Place in a bowl and toss with half of the dressing.

Arrange the cheese rounds on a baking (cookie) sheet and bake for 10 minutes or until crispy.

Divide the rocket (arugula), beetroot and goat's cheese rounds among individual plates and drizzle remaining dressing over the salad. Serve immediately while warm.

GET ORGANIZED

Beetroot tastes best prepared on the day of serving but could be roasted the day before. The goat's cheese cakes and dressing can be prepared the day before and stored in the refrigerator.

VARIATIONS

If you don't want to go to the trouble of making the goat's cheese cakes, you could spread goat's cheese on some crostini and put it under the grill (broiler). Sherry Vinegar and Walnut Oil Vinaigrette (see page 60) would be lovely in place of the balsamic dressing. Blanched fine green beans could also be added.

baby beetroot (beets)
with red wine vinegar, garlic and parsley

Beetroot (beet) is notable for its earthy taste and dramatic purple colour. Baby beetroot are much sweeter than their larger siblings, but if you can't get them, just quarter the larger ones before roasting. This mouth-puckering dressing is my favourite, but you substitute any vinaigrette that you particularly like.

You can boil or roast the beetroot (beets). Trim off the tops, but do not cut below the skin. Leave the base intact.

To boil, fill a large pan with salted water, add the beetroot and bring to the boil. Cook until easily pierced with knife.

To roast, heat the oven to 200°C/400°F/Gas Mark 6. Place the beetroot in a large piece of foil and sprinkle with olive oil, salt and pepper. Wrap tightly and place in the oven for 30 minutes or until easily pierced.

Meanwhile, whisk together the vinegar, oil, parsley and garlic in a bowl and set aside.

When the beetroot is cooked, leave to cool slightly, then wearing rubber (latex) gloves to protect your hands, peel them. Halve, then quarter, baby beetroot or slice the larger ones into 1 cm/½ inch pieces.

Pour the dressing over the beetroot while they are still warm. This salad is delicious served warm or at room temperature.

SERVES 6 (APPETIZER), 4 (MAIN COURSE) OR 8 (SIDE DISH)

PREPARATION TIME: 30 MINUTES

8 small beetroot (beets) or 4 medium to large beetroot, scrubbed

1 tsp salt

3 tbsp olive oil (optional)

½ tsp freshly ground black pepper

3 tbsp red wine vinegar

4 tbsp extra virgin olive oil

20g/¾ oz/¾ cup fresh flat leaf parsley, chopped

1 garlic clove, finely chopped

GET ORGANIZED

This salad will keep fresh for 24 hours in the refrigerator, but bring it back to room temperature before serving.

VARIATIONS

Substitute Balsamic Dressing (see page 152), or Sherry Vinegar and Walnut Oil Vinaigrette (see page 60). You could also make a tasty dressing by mixing together 1 tbsp freshly grated or prepared horseradish, 1 tsp lemon juice, 4 tbsp sour cream and ½ tsp each salt and black pepper. Chopped red onion or other vegetables such as green and yellow beans would be tasty additions.

char-grilled courgette (zucchini)
and pepper salad with feta, mint and balsamic dressing

This recipe was inspired by Sophie Grigson's book, Eat Your Greens. Grilled courgettes (zucchini) and roasted (bell) peppers are tossed in a garlicky balsamic dressing while still warm and then sprinkled with feta cheese and fresh, cool mint. Wonderful served warm in the winter and refreshing at room temperature in summer.

SERVES 6 (APPETIZER),
4 (MAIN COURSE) OR
8 (SIDE DISH)

PREPARATION TIME:
25 MINUTES

**4 red (bell) peppers,
de-seeded and cut
into quarters**

**4 medium courgettes
(zucchini), cut lengthways
into 1 cm/½ inch thick slices**

4 tbsp olive oil

1 tsp sea salt

**1 tsp freshly ground
black pepper**

**1 quantity Balsamic Dressing
(see page 152)**

2 tbsp chopped fresh mint

**200 g/7 oz feta cheese,
crumbled**

Heat the grill (broiler). Arrange the (bell) pepper quarters, skin side up, in a large roasting pan. Place under grill (broiler) until blackened. Transfer to a plastic bag and seal.

Place the courgette (zucchini) slices in the same pan. Toss with the olive oil and sprinkle with salt and pepper. Place under grill (broiler) until crisp, turning them over so that both sides are browned. (Alternatively, you can use a stove-top grill pan to grill the courgettes (zucchini).) Remove the slices from the pan and place in large bowl.

Peel the peppers and cut the quarters into large pieces. Add them to the courgettes (zucchini).

Place all of the dressing ingredients in a screw-top jar and shake well. Pour the dressing over the vegetables while they are still warm and sprinkle the mint on top.

Just before serving, sprinkle each portion with feta.

If serving hot, then place in an ovenproof dish under the grill and briefly brown the cheese.

GET ORGANIZED

Vegetables can be grilled in the morning and the dressing can be made the day before. If preparing ahead, pour only half of the dressing over the warm vegetables and add the mint, feta and remaining dressing just before serving.

VARIATIONS

Gorgonzola or other blue cheese may be used instead of feta.

pan-fried halloumi cheese,

asparagus and citrus caper vinaigrette

This Cypriot cheese, with its elastic texture, is ideal for char-grilling or pan-frying. Apart from its flavour, the most exciting thing about halloumi is that it keeps in it's water-packed bag in the refrigerator for almost a year. Pull it out for an impromptu appetizer and pair with any piquant dressing.

SERVES 6 (APPETIZER), 4 (MAIN COURSE) OR 8 (SIDE DISH)

PREPARATION TIME: 20 MINUTES

1 bunch of thin asparagus, trimmed

1 quantity Citrus Caper Vinaigrette (see page 150)

2 blood or navel oranges

250 g/8 oz halloumi cheese, drained and cut into 8 slices

125 g/4 oz/1 cup plain (all-purpose) flour

1 tsp each salt and freshly ground black pepper

2 tbsp olive oil

Cook the asparagus in salted, boiling water until al dente. Drain and plunge into iced water, then pat dry and arrange on large platter or individual plates.

Put all the vinaigrette ingredients into a screw-top jar, shake well and set aside.

Cut off the rind from the oranges and cut the flesh into 1 cm/½ inch slices. Cut the slices in half and place on the asparagus.

Dust the halloumi slices with flour and season with salt and pepper.

Heat the olive oil in sauté pan until very hot. Brown the halloumi until crispy on both sides. Remove and arrange on asparagus.

Drizzle the vinaigrette over the salad and serve straight away.

GET ORGANIZED

The asparagus, orange slices, and vinaigrette can be prepared in the morning. The halloumi shouldn't be fried until just before serving.

VARIATIONS

Halloumi could be used with the dressing on it's own without oranges or asparagus. Green beans or cherry tomatoes could be used in place of the asparagus. Harissa Dressing (see page 151) or Anchovy, Caper and Garlic Dressing (see page 150) could replace the vinaigrette.

warm salad of green beans,

poached egg and ravigote dressing

I live near a heavenly French brasserie called Brula. This is one of their signature appetizers, for which the partner Lawrence has kindly given me the recipe. To fully appreciate it, enjoy with a glass of chilled white Burgundy.

SERVES 4 (APPETIZER)

PREPARATION TIME: 30 MINUTES

200 g/7 oz green beans, trimmed

1 tbsp olive oil

1 tbsp white wine vinegar

4 free-range (farm-fresh) eggs

FOR THE DRESSING

2 tsp Dijon mustard

1 tsp red wine vinegar

½ tsp each of salt and freshly ground black pepper

175 ml/6 fl oz/¾ cup groundnut (peanut) oil

1 tbsp capers, rinsed and chopped

1 tbsp finely chopped fresh flat leaf parsley

2 finely chopped fresh tarragon sprigs

1 tbsp finely chopped shallot

Blanch the beans in salted, boiling water until al dente. Drain and immediately plunge into iced water. This will help retain their green colour.

For the dressing. Whisk together the mustard, vinegar, salt and pepper in a small bowl. Gradually whisk in the oil. Stir in the capers, herbs and shallot.

Just before serving, gently heat the beans with the olive oil in a pan.

Meanwhile, bring 1 litre/1¾ pints/4 cups water to the boil with the vinegar, then cook 1 egg at a time. Crack an egg into a cup, quickly swirl the boiling water with a spoon and then gently slide the egg into the centre of the swirling water and poach for 3–5 minutes. Carefully remove with a slotted spoon and drain on a tea towel (dishtowel).

Divide the beans among individual serving plates, place a poached egg on each and drizzle the dressing over the salads.

GET ORGANIZED

The beans can be cooked in the morning. The dressing can also be made in the morning but will lose its green colour after 3–4 hours.

VARIATIONS

Artichoke bottoms could replace the beans. Slices of rare beef or crispy bacon would make a tasty addition. Other vinegars could be used in the dressing, such as sherry or white wine.

crispy aubergine (eggplant),
spring onion (scallion) and chilli salad
with sweet soy, ginger and chilli dressing

SERVES 6 (APPETIZER),
4 (MAIN COURSE) OR
8 (SIDE DISH)

PREPARATION TIME:
40 MINUTES

4 spring onions (scallions), cut into thin julienne

2 thumb-size red chillies, cut into thin julienne

3 small to medium aubergines (eggplant)

1 litre/1¾ pints/4 cups groundnut (peanut) or vegetable oil

1 quantity Sweet Soy, Ginger and Chilli Dressing (see page 153)

1 small bunch of fresh coriander (cilantro)

After a brilliant lunch at E & O restaurant in Notting Hill, London, I was spurred into making my own version of their exalted aubergine (eggplant) salad with soy. After repeated attempts roasting and grilling, I realized that frying the aubergines is essential. Groundnut (peanut) oil is best, giving crispy results without leaving a heavy deep-fried odour.

Place the spring onions (scallions) and chillies in bowl of water and chill in the refrigerator until required. This makes them crisp and sweeter in taste.

Cut the aubergines (eggplant) into 1 cm/½ inch thick slices. Heat the oil in wok or heavy-based pan. It is ready for frying when a piece of bread added to it sizzles immediately. Deep-fry the aubergines until brown and crispy, then drain on kitchen paper (paper towels). Arrange the aubergine slices in a large bowl.

Place all the dressing ingredients in a small bowl and mix well. Alternatively, pulse them in a food processor.

Drain the spring onions and chillies and sprinkle them over the aubergines. Pour the dressing over the salad and serve immediately, garnished with fresh coriander (cilantro) leaves.

GET ORGANIZED

The dressing can be made the day before, but the salad should be served within 2 hours of preparation.

VARIATIONS

Thai Chilli Lime Dressing (see page 153) or Miso Dressing (see page 153) could be used in place of the soy dressing for a South-east Asian version.

farmers' market salad
with croutons and goat's cheese

Every afternoon, while staying at a villa in Crete with my family, I made a large lunch salad, using fresh ingredients from the local market. This is the result. Although Greeks would use creamy Myzithra cheese, mild goat's cheese works just as well.

**SERVES 6 (APPETIZER),
4 (MAIN COURSE) OR
8 (SIDE DISH)**

**PREPARATION TIME:
20 MINUTES**

**½ stick sourdough or
French bread cut into
1 cm/½ inch cubes**

**300 g/11 oz ripe cherry
or pomodorino tomatoes,
halved**

**1 large red onion,
finely chopped**

**3 Lebanese cucumbers, sliced,
or 1 large cucumber, peeled,
seeded and sliced**

20 black olives, pitted

**2 tbsp chopped fresh oregano
or 2 tsp dried oregano**

**1 quantity Anchovy, Caper
and Garlic Dressing
(see page 150)**

**150 g/5 oz mild goat's
cheese, crumbled**

Heat the oven to 200°C/400°F/Gas Mark 6.

Spread out the bread cubes on a baking (cookie) sheet and brown in the oven for about 8 minutes. Leave to cool, then place in a large serving bowl.

Add the tomatoes, onion, cucumbers, olives and oregano.

Place all the dressing ingredients in a screw-top jar and shake well.

Just before serving add the dressing to the salad and mix well. Sprinkle the goat's cheese over it and serve.

GET ORGANIZED

The croûtons can be prepared 2 days ahead and stored in an airtight container. The dressing can be made the day before. The vegetables can be cut up on the day, but do not add the onion until 1 hour before serving.

VARIATIONS

Fresh dill could replace the oregano. Other crunchy vegetables, such as radishes, red (bell) pepper or celery, could be added. Served with slices of chicken, lamb or rare beef, this salad would make a delicious meal on its own. Capers or caper berries could be used to garnish.

warm baby artichokes
with cherry tomatoes and olives

SERVES 6 (APPETIZER),
4 (MAIN COURSE) OR
8 (SIDE DISH)

PREPARATION TIME:
50 MINUTES

2 lemons, halved

16 baby artichokes

1 large onion, finely chopped

1 large carrot, finely chopped

4 garlic cloves,
finely chopped

4 tbsp olive oil

1 tsp each salt and
black pepper

1 small handful of fresh
basil, chopped

1 tbsp chopped fresh thyme

2 tbsp chopped fresh parsley

5 tbsp red wine vinegar

2 tbsp clear honey

250 ml/8 fl oz/1 cup
white wine

350 ml/12 fl oz/1½ cups
chicken stock

6 cherry tomatoes, halved

10 mild-flavoured black olives

2 large handfuls of rocket
(arugula), to serve

I discovered this recipe at Roger Verge's cooking school in Mougin, southern France. The artichokes cook in a divine sauce of mirepoix, red wine vinegar, honey and fresh herbs. Baby artichokes are easiest to use as their undeveloped chokes just need a little trimming. They're seasonal in spring and autumn (fall), so scoop them up as soon as you see them.

Fill a large bowl with water and squeeze in the lemons into water. Using a paring knife, trim the stems of artichokes, leaving 2.5 cm/1 inch remaining. Trim off the tough leaves, turning as you cut. Cut 2.5 cm/1 inch off top of each artichoke. Using a melon baller, scoop out the fuzzy chokes inside. If you are using very small baby artichokes, then that won't be necessary. Using a vegetable peeler, peel off remaining hard parts near the base of the stems. As you finish preparing each artichoke, drop it into the acidulated water.

Put the onion, carrot, garlic and olive oil in a large pan. Sprinkle with salt and pepper and cook gently over a medium heat for 5 minutes.

Drain and add the artichokes to the pan of vegetables, then add the herbs, vinegar, honey, wine and chicken stock. Cover and cook over a medium high heat for 6 minutes, then lower the heat to medium and cook for 12 minutes more.

Remove the lid from the pan, add the tomatoes and olives and cook over a low heat 5 minutes.

Place some rocket (arugula) on each plate or a large platter. Scoop artichokes on top and serve warm, with bread.

GET ORGANIZED

This can be prepared in the morning, but do not add the olives and tomatoes until just before serving.

VARIATIONS

Add other spring vegetables, such as fresh peas, asparagus or fine green beans.

barbecued marinated portabello mushrooms
with gorgonzola

Meaty portabello mushrooms absorb marinades without becoming too soggy. After they're bathed in a herb-drenched vinaigrette and barbecued, they are topped with creamy Gorgonzola cheese.

SERVES 6 (APPETIZER),
4 (MAIN COURSE) OR
8 (SIDE DISH)

PREPARATION TIME:
20 MINUTES

**8 large portabello or
field mushrooms**

**3 garlic cloves,
finely chopped**

**small handful of fresh mint
leaves, chopped**

**small handful of fresh basil
leaves, chopped**

1 tsp salt

freshly ground black pepper

3 tbsp sherry vinegar

4 tbsp balsamic vinegar

**125 ml/4 fl oz/½ cup extra
virgin olive oil**

**100 g/31/2 oz Gorgonzola
cheese, cut into 1 cm/
½ inch cubes**

**radicchio or rocket (arugula)
leaves, to serve**

Lightly score a criss-cross pattern into the tops of the mushroom caps and arrange the mushrooms in shallow dish.

Combine the garlic, herbs, salt, pepper, both kinds of vinegar and olive oil in a small bowl. Stir well and pour the mixture over the mushrooms. Set aside to marinate for at least 10 minutes and up to 30 minutes. Don't leave to marinate for too long or the mushrooms will become soggy.

Cook the mushrooms on a hot barbecue or under a heated grill (broiler) until brown on both sides.

Just before serving, spoon a little cheese on to the stem side of each mushroom cap. Return to the heat until the cheese has melted.

Serve immediately on radicchio or rocket (arugula).

GET ORGANIZED

The marinade ingredients can be combined in the morning, but the mushrooms shouldn't be marinated until 30 minutes before cooking.

VARIATIONS

Mascarpone or goat's cheese could replace the Gorgonzola with very decadent results. Crostini could be served under the mushrooms to make the salad more substantial.

warm salad of pumpkin with mint,
red onion and sweet and sour vinaigrette

Creamy pumpkin is roasted, then drizzled with a warm, sweet and sour dressing of chillies, garlic and mint. Use a firm-fleshed variety such as Jamaican – an enormous pumpkin sold in chunks at food markets. Other types are stringy and watery, not providing the necessary velvety texture. Butternut squash is an excellent substitute.

Heat the oven to 200°C/400°F/Gas Mark 6.

Place pumpkin cubes on a large baking (cookie) sheet. Toss with 2 tbsp of the olive oil and season with the salt and pepper. Bake, shaking the baking sheet occasionally, for 20 minutes or until golden and tender.

Heat the remaining oil in a sauté pan. Add the garlic and cook until golden brown. Pour in the vinegar and add the honey, onion and chilli. Bring to the boil, then lower the heat and simmer for 5 minutes until syrupy.

Transfer the warm pumpkin to a large dish. When ready to serve, drizzle the warm dressing over it and sprinkle with chopped mint.

Place some rocket (arugula) leaves on each plate, spoon pumpkin on top and sprinkle with the pine nuts.

SERVES 6 (APPETIZER), 4 (MAIN COURSE) OR 8 (SIDE DISH)

PREPARATION TIME: 40 MINUTES

1 kg/2¼ lb pumpkin or butternut squash, peeled and cut into 2.5 cm/1 inch cubes

5 tbsp extra virgin olive oil

1 tsp salt

1 tsp freshly ground black pepper

2 garlic cloves, thinly sliced

3 tbsp red wine vinegar

1½ tbsp clear honey

1 small red onion, thinly sliced

½ tsp crushed dried red chilli

2 tbsp chopped fresh mint

4 handfuls of rocket (arugula)

4 tbsp pine nuts, toasted

GET ORGANIZED

The pumpkin or squash can be prepared at least 2 hours ahead. Undercook, immediately place in the refrigerator and finish off cooking just before serving. The dressing can be made in the morning.

VARIATIONS

Use (bell) peppers, sweet potatoes, or courgettes (zucchini) in place of the pumpkin or butternut squash. Prawns (shrimp), Garlic Croûtons (see page 156) or black olives would be tasty additions.

oodles of noodles
and rice

6

Slippery, salty and oh so
sensational, noodles and rice
will never leave you bored.
Both are akin to exotic Asian
or Mediterranean tastes, making
the possibilities endless. Over
indulging is not uncommon and
can be a frequent affliction
associated with them. Eating them
with chopsticks is probably a skill you're
born with so don't be ashamed to pick up
a fork — it's faster anyway. Perfect salad for
picnics, lunches or greedy dinners by yourself.

Asian noodle know-how

Supreme in Asian culture and cuisine, noodles are eaten enthusiastically for breakfast, lunch and dinner. Heads bowed over bowls of noodles is a familiar sight all over Asia. Fat, skinny, round or flat, noodles make intruiging salads tossed with soy or lime dressings. The numerous types and shapes of noodles can be overwhelming, so use this guide to make sure that you're getting the right one. Let your intuition guide you on added ingredients. Seared duck breast, seafood, chillies, spring onions (scallions) and julienne vegetables are just a few, but let your creativity flow.

WHEAT NOODLES

Made from a flour and water base, these sometimes include egg as well. All of these varieties need to be boiled before using. Most can be purchased in the Asian section of a supermarket.

Chinese egg noodles (2) – Bright yellow noodles found fat or thin and produced in fresh and dried form. Hearty additions such as spicy peanut sauce, seared duck or shredded pork work well with them.

Chinese wheat noodles – Mainly sold dried in individual "nest" portions at Chinese food stores. The size varies from thin to thick and they made round or flat. Toss with an Asian pesto or other vibrant dressings.

Ramen noodles (5) – Pale yellow Japanese egg noodles. Sold fresh or dried in Japanese food stores. Not my first choice for salad, but could be used in place of other egg noodles.

Somen noodles (7) – Elegant in their ribbon-tied bundles, these delicate thin, white noodles are from Japan. Best served simply with a soy dressing or tossed with chilli, ginger and coriander (cilantro).

Udon noodles (8) – Fat, white Japanese noodles sold fresh in vacuum packs or dried. Manufactured round, square or flat, they are well suited for soy-ginger dressings, chillies and spring onions (scallions). Good side salad for grilled (broiled) Asian pork or braised pork belly (side).

RICE NOODLES

Produced from rice starch or rice flour, these noodles should be soaked in very hot water until soft. The soaking time will vary according to the thickness. Although they are appearing more often in grocery stores, you may need to visit an Asian store to find them.

Rice sticks (6) – Similar to vermicelli in taste and texture, rice sticks are flatter and have a wider variety of sizes. They range from very thin (similar to vermicelli), medium (fettuccine-size), all the way to large flat Thai noodles called jantaboon. The thin and medium sizes are best for salads and versatile with Thai, Chinese and Vietnamese flavours.

Thin rice vermicelli noodles (9) – Tiny thread noodles used by the Chinese, Thais and Vietnamese. Sold in tidy bundles or thick crinkled rafts, they are among the best noodles for salads. Their bland nature is perfect for soaking up big flavours such as garlic, chillies and ginger. Not only used soft, they are excellent deep-fried for crunchy texture.

BEAN THREAD NOODLES

Visit a Thai or Chinese store to find these noodles made from mung bean starch. Soak for in hot water before using.

Glass noodles (3) – Also called cellophane noodles, they are valued for their transparent appearance after soaking. These fine noodles are particularly good with a lime juice and Thai fish sauce dressing, and punchy Asian herbs such as mint, coriander (cilantro) and Thai basil. They make delicious vegetarian salads and can also be mixed with paper-thin slices of seared beef, flakes of crab or juicy prawns (shrimp).

BUCKWHEAT NOODLES

These protein-rich noodles are made from buckwheat and can be found in supermarkets and Japanese food stores. Boil them for 1–2 minutes before using.

Green tea noodles (4) – Also called *chasoba* noodles, these Japanese noodles are soba noodles with green tea flavouring. Their pale moss-green colour and green tea taste make interesting salads. Seared beef, teriyaki, asparagus, duck and spring onions (scallions) all complement them well.

Soba noodles (1) – Pale brown Japanese noodles sold dried, in packets, similar to spaghetti. Their sturdy texture and nutty taste produce outstanding salads. Serve traditionally, chilled on ice with dashi dipping sauce or tossed with soy, garlic and crispy vegetables such as broccoli.

Thai glass noodles with asian herbs,
crispy shallots and chilli lime dressing

Glistening noodles with aromatic herbs, sweet and sour lime dressing and crispy fried shallots – pure bliss. Refreshing for summer lunch or as a light appetizer for an Asian dinner, this also makes a brilliant base for seared tuna slices, prawns (shrimp) or crab.

SERVES 6 (APPETIZER), 4 (MAIN COURSE) OR 8 (SIDE DISH)

PREPARATION TIME: 1 HOUR

150 g/5 oz very thin glass (cellophane or mung bean) noodles

1 carrot, cut into julienne

1 medium red onion, finely diced

5 cm/2 inch piece of fresh root ginger, cut into thin julienne

1 large handful of fresh Thai sweet basil leaves or other basil leaves

1 handful of fresh coriander (cilantro) leaves

15 fresh mint leaves

1 quantity Thai Chilli Lime Dressing (see page 153)

1 quantity Crispy Shallots (see page 156)

2 tbsp crushed salted peanuts or cashew nuts

1 quantity Fried Ginger Sticks (see page 157) (optional)

Soak the noodles in boiling water for about 5 minutes or until al dente. Drain and rinse in cold water. Dry on a tea towel (dishtowel). Using a pair of scissors, cut the noodles into 6 inch lengths so that it is easier to mix. (The Chinese consider it bad luck to do this, but after doing this numerous times, nothing detrimental has happened to me!)

Place the noodles, carrot, onion, fresh ginger, basil, coriander (cilantro) and mint in a bowl.

Pour all the dressing ingredients into screw-top jar, shake well and pour it over the salad. (Alternatively, crush the dressing ingredients in a mortar and pestle, adding the lime juice and fish sauce last.)

Arrange the salad on a large platter with the crispy shallots, crushed peanuts and fried ginger sticks, if using.

GET ORGANIZED

The dressing, shallots and vegetables can be prepared the night before and stored in airtight containers. Do not add the onion until 2 hours before serving.

VARIATIONS

Prawns (shrimp), crab, lobster, seared slices of tuna, shredded chicken, or seared fillet (tenderloin) of beef would all be tasty additions.

soba noodles with garlic broccoli
and sweet soy, ginger and chilli dressing

Soba are buckwheat noodles from Japan that have a distinctive nutty flavour. Traditionally, the Japanese serve them plain with a soy dipping sauce, but I find them even more glorious with a ginger dressing and crunchy, sprouting broccoli. Look for sweet soy sauce, called "kecap manis", in the Asian section of the supermarket, ethnic food internet sites or Chinese food stores.

SERVES 6 (APPETIZER), 4 (MAIN COURSE) OR 8 (SIDE DISH)

PREPARATION TIME: 20 MINUTES

250 g/8 oz Japanese soba or somen noodles

350 g/12 oz purple sprouting or regular broccoli, cut into 2.5 cm/1 inch pieces

salt

1 quantity Sweet Soy, Ginger and Chilli Dressing (see page 152)

2 tbsp vegetable oil

1 garlic clove, thinly sliced

1 tbsp toasted sesame seeds

Cook the noodles in boiling water for 5 minutes or until al dente. Soba noodles cook very quickly so check them regularly. Drain and immerse in iced water. Drain again and dry on a tea towel (dishtowel).

Cook the broccoli in salted, boiling water until al dente. Drain and immerse immediately in iced water. Drain again and dry on tea towels.

Place all dressing ingredients in food processor and pulse. Alternatively, chop them by hand.

Place the noodles in a large bowl. Pour the dressing over them, mix well and set aside.

Heat the vegetable oil in large sauté pan, add the garlic and cook until golden.

Add the broccoli, sear in the hot oil for 2–3 minutes and then toss into the bowl with the noodles. Mix well, sprinkle with sesame seeds and serve.

GET ORGANIZED

The salad can be fully prepared no more than 4 hours before serving. If left longer the noodles will become too starchy. Hold back dressing until serving.

VARIATIONS

Thin slices of beef fillet, sirloin, prawns (shrimp) or shredded poached chicken would suit well.

green tea noodles with soy duck
and tamarind and lemon grass dressing

Fusion cuisine is exciting with its melange of flavours, but there is a fine line when it becomes "confusion" cooking. This combines lots of punchy tastes without being overdone. Noodles are tossed with a tamarind and lemon grass dressing, seared soy duck and sprinkled with fried shallots and ginger sticks. Green tea noodles are Japanese buckwheat soba with green tea flavouring. Their unique moss green colour and taste make exciting salads. Use any other noodles, such as somen, egg noodle or soba.

SERVES 6 (APPETIZER), 4 (MAIN COURSE) OR 8 (SIDE DISH)

PREPARATION TIME: 40 MINUTES, PLUS 2 HOURS FOR MARINATING

4 duck breasts

1 tbsp Thai fish sauce

4 tbsp soy sauce

2 tbsp clear honey

½ tsp each salt and black pepper

250 g/8 oz green tea soba or other Asian noodles

1 quantity Crispy Shallots (see page 156)

1 quantity Fried Ginger Sticks (see page 157)

1 quantity Tamarind and Lemon Grass Dressing (see page 151)

2 carrots, cut into thin julienne

5 spring onions (scallions), thinly sliced

10 fresh baby corn, sliced lengthways and boiled

15 g/½ oz/½ cup fresh coriander (cilantro) leaves

15g/1½ oz/1½ cup fresh mint leaves

Using a sharp knife, score a criss-cross pattern across the fat side of the duck breasts. Place them in a shallow glass or ceramic dish and drizzle with the Thai fish sauce, soy sauce and honey. Mix well and season with salt and pepper. Set aside in the refrigerator to marinate for 2 hours.

Heat the oven to 200°C/400°F/Gas Mark 6.

Cook the noodles in boiling salted water until al dente. Drain and immerse in iced water, then leave until required.

Prepare the dressing, crispy shallots and fried ginger sticks and set aside.

Drain the duck breasts and dry thoroughly on kitchen paper (paper towels).

Heat a sauté pan until very hot. Quickly sear the duck on both sides, then reduce the heat to low. Cook, fat side down, for about 10 minutes until most of the fat has rendered. This will produce a thin crispy skin.

Transfer the duck to a shallow roasting pan and cook in the oven for 10 minutes.

Remove the duck from oven and set aside to rest for 10 minutes, then thinly slice the meat.

Drain the noodles and dry on a tea towel (dishtowel), then place them in a large mixing bowl.

Add the carrots, spring onions (scallions), baby corn, coriander (cilantro), mint and duck slices. Pour the dressing over the salad and sprinkle with the shallots and ginger sticks.

GET ORGANIZED

The duck can be marinated overnight. The salad is best prepared the hour before eating or the noodles become starchy.

VARIATIONS

Seared beef or prawns (shrimp) could replace duck. A Thai Chilli Lime Dressing (see page 153) could be used in place of the tamarind.

crispy rice stick noodles
with Thai chicken

SERVES 6 (APPETIZER), 4 (MAIN COURSE) OR 8 (SIDE DISH)

PREPARATION TIME: 25 MINUTES

600 ml/1 pint/2½ cups groundnut (peanut) oil or vegetable oil for frying

100 g/3½ oz rice stick noodles or thin vermicelli rice noodles, broken into 5 cm/2 inch lengths

6 skinless, boneless chicken breasts

1 large red onion, finely chopped

3 tbsp grated fresh root ginger

2 small red chillies, de-seeded and chopped

1 large handful of fresh coriander (cilantro), finely chopped

½ iceberg lettuce, core removed and leaves separated

fresh coriander leaves, to garnish

FOR THE DRESSING

4 tbsp fresh lime juice

125 ml/4 fl oz/½ cup fresh lemon juice

4 tbsp Thai fish sauce

2 tbsp sugar

2 tbsp water

Heat the oil in a wok or large, heavy pan until a piece of noodle sizzles immediately it is added to the pan. Cook the noodles, in batches if necessary, remove with a wire scoop and drain on kitchen paper (paper towels).

Place the chicken breasts in a food processor and pulse until minced (ground).

Discard all but 3 tbsp of the oil from the wok or pan. Re-heat over medium high heat until almost smoking. Add the chicken and cook until browned, breaking it up thoroughly with a large fork. If chicken gives off too much liquid, tilt the pan and spoon it out.

Transfer the chicken to a bowl, add the onion, ginger, chillies and coriander (cilantro) and toss well.

For the dressing. Combine the lime juice, lemon juice, Thai fish sauce, sugar and water in a screw-top jar and shake well. Toss the salad with dressing. Season with more Thai fish sauce, if necessary.

Pile a couple of lettuce leaves on top of each other to make individual "bowls". Spoon the fried noodles and chicken salad into each bowl, sprinkle a few coriander leaves over the top and serve.

GET ORGANIZED

The dressing and pan-fried chicken can made in the morning and stored in the refrigerator. The noodles can be fried the day before and stored in an airtight container. The salad shouldn't be assembled more than 1 hour before eating, otherwise the onion may dominate the flavour and it will become soggy.

VARIATIONS

Julienne carrots or red (bell) peppers would be a colourful addition. Instead of iceberg lettuce "bowls", serve on a bed of chopped Cos or romaine hearts.

arborio rice with spring vegetables,
dill and red wine vinaigrette

My sister Teresa makes a delicious concoction called Confetti Rice Salad. I have modified her idea slightly by using arborio rice with spring vegetables. Arborio is a stubby flat rice that is mainly used to make risotto. Far heartier than standard rice, it will retain its texture without going soggy.

Cook the rice in boiling water until al dente. Drain, rinse with cold water and drain again, then place in a large mixing bowl.

Blanch the peas, asparagus and beans in separate pans of salted water until al dente. Drain and immediately immerse in iced water. Drain and dry on tea towels (dishtowels) and place in the bowl with the rice.

Add the onion, spring onions (scallions), artichokes, (bell) pepper, olives, dill, parsley and mint.

Combine all the vinaigrette ingredients in a screw-top jar, shake well and pour the dressing over the salad. Combine well, taste and add more salt and vinegar, if necessary, and serve.

SERVES 6 APPETIZER, 4 (MAIN COURSE) OR 8 (SIDE DISH)

PREPARATION TIME: 30 MINUTES

250 g/8 oz arborio rice

125 g/4 oz/1 cup shelled fresh or frozen peas

1 bunch of thin asparagus, trimmed and cut into 2.5 cm/1 inch pieces

100 g/3½ oz/1 cup fine green beans, trimmed

salt

1 medium red onion, finely chopped

4 spring onions (scallions), finely chopped

200 g/7 oz jar artichokes, drained and cut into quarters

1 red (bell) pepper, de-seeded and finely chopped

20 black olives, pitted and halved

2 tbsp finely chopped fresh dill

2 tbsp finely chopped fresh flat leaf parsley

2 tbsp finely chopped fresh mint

1 quantity Classic Red Wine Vinaigrette (see page 150)

GET ORGANIZED

The dressed salad will keep for 4 hours, but do not add the onion until 1 hour before serving. The dressing, blanched vegetables and pasta can be prepared in the morning and stored in the refrigerator.

VARIATIONS

Orzo or other small pasta could be used in place of the rice. Cooked fresh baby artichokes would be much better than bottled if you have time to prepare them. Shelled broad (fava) beans could be added.

gigli with chicken,
olives, (bell) peppers, capers and sweet and spicy vinaigrette

Most pasta salads are uninspiring, but this one holds the promise of an idyllic summer lunch. Juicy shreds of chicken and pasta are fused with punchy capers, olives, fresh basil and a sweet vinegary dressing.

SERVES 6 (APPETIZER), 4 (MAIN COURSE) OR 8 (SIDE DISH)

PREPARATION TIME: 40 MINUTES

100g/3½ oz gigli or penne pasta

salt

500 ml/18 fl oz/2¼ cups chicken stock

4 skinless, boneless chicken breasts

1 red (bell) pepper, de-seeded and cut into thin julienne

1 yellow (bell) pepper, de-seeded and cut into thin julienne

1 small red onion, finely diced

20 peppadew, pepperoncini or other sweet pickled peppers, de-seeded and cut into 1 cm/½ inch rings

4 sun blush or good quality sun-dried tomatoes (packed in olive oil), finely chopped

100 g/3½ oz cherry tomatoes, mixed colours and shapes (pomodorino, pear drop, yellow, etc.), halved

1 tbsp tiny capers, rinsed

20 black olives, pitted

25 g/1 oz/1 cup fresh basil, finely chopped

1 quantity Sweet and Spicy Vinaigrette (see page 150)

Cook the pasta in salted, boiling water until al dente. Drain and rinse with cold water. Drain well again and place in large bowl.

Bring the stock to the boil in a medium pan. Add the chicken and then turn off the heat. Cover and leave to stand for 30 minutes. Alternatively you can sear or char-grill the chicken, but it will be slightly drier.

Remove the chicken from the stock, shred into pieces and add to the pasta.

Add the (bell) peppers, onion, pickled peppers, both kinds of tomatoes, capers, olives, and basil to the bowl.

Place all the vinaigrette ingredients in a screw-top jar and shake well. Pour the dressing over the salad and mix together. Serve at room temperature.

GET ORGANIZED

The dressing, poached chicken and chopped vegetables can be prepared the night before and stored in the refrigerator. The salad can be assembled 2 hours before serving.

VARIATIONS

Marinated artichokes, palm hearts or celery could all be added.

shredded chicken and lemon grass rice salad

SERVES 6 (APPETIZER),
4 (MAIN COURSE) OR
8 (SIDE DISH)

PREPARATION TIME:
30 MINUTES

1 kg/2¼ lb chicken or
4 chicken breasts

400 g/14 oz/2 cups rice,
preferably Thai jasmine

2 lemon grass stalks (lower
portion only, outer leaves
removed), finely chopped

2 small red chillies, de-seeded
and finely chopped

20 g/3/4 oz/¾ cup shredded
fresh mint

20 g/3/4 oz/¾ cup fresh
coriander (cilantro)

3 kaffir lime leaves (optional)

1 small red onion,
finely diced

2 x quantity Thai Chilli Lime
Dressing (see page 153)

Get your picnic basket ready for a salad bursting with fresh Thai flavours. Poaching whole chicken or chicken breasts guarantees that the meat will be juicy and tender.

Bring large pan of water to the boil. Add the whole chicken or the chicken breasts and cook for 10 minutes. Turn off the heat, cover and leave the whole chicken to stand for 1 hour or the chicken breasts the stand for 15 minutes.

Remove the chicken to a plate and leave to cool slightly, then discard the skin and bones. Shred the meat and set aside.

Cook the rice in plenty of boiling water until tender but still firm. Drain and rinse in cold water. Drain again and set aside.

Place the rice, chicken, mint, coriander (cilantro), lime leaves, chopped red onion, chillies and lemon grass into a bowl and toss to combine.

Put all the dressing ingredients into a screw-top jar, shake well and pour it over the salad. Taste and add more lime juice or Thai fish sauce, if necessary.

Chill until ready to serve.

VARIATIONS

Poached prawns (shrimp), crab, lobster, or beef fillet (tenderloin) slices could be used in place of the chicken. Julienne of carrot or red (bell) pepper would be colourful additions. Any type of rice could be used – black rice looks especially dramatic.

spicy peanut noodles

SERVES 6 (APPETIZER),
4 (MAIN COURSE) OR
8 (SIDE DISH)

PREPARATION TIME:
15 MINUTES

450 g/1 lb thin vermicelli or
penne pasta

salt

200 g/7 oz can water
chestnuts, drained and
thinly sliced

8 spring onions (scallions),
thinly sliced

FOR THE DRESSING

175 ml/6 fl oz/¾ cup crunchy
peanut butter

4 tbsp chilli oil

4 tbsp sesame oil

3 tbsp sugar

4 tbsp soy sauce

4 tbsp red wine vinegar

4 tbsp cold water

2 tbsp hot chilli bean paste

Plan to overindulge when making these.

Cook the pasta in salted, boiling water until al dente. Drain and place in a large mixing bowl.

For the dressing. Using a whisk, mix all the dressing ingredients together in small bowl until smooth.

Add the dressing to the pasta while warm and mix well.

When the pasta has begun to cool slightly, add the water chestnuts and spring onions (scallions).

Serve while still warm or cool to room temperature.

something substantial –
meat, fish and poultry

7

No other courses are required here;
you will get all the fulfilment you
need. Flaky crab, crispy quail or
char-grilled beef elevate salad to
a different level. Meat, fish and
poultry are the celebrities and
the lettuce quietly blends in.
Enhance their depth with spices
and marinades, making the wafting
fragrance in your kitchen
even more irresistible.

crispy quail, char-grilled aubergines (eggplant) and green beans with pomegranate dressing

There is something slightly comical about grilled quail with their Lilliputian wings and gloriously tiny thighs. Save yourself aggravation by asking your butcher to bone them. Pomegranate molasses is an Iranian import made from boiled, crushed pomegranate seeds. Not only used for vinaigrettes, its sticky essence is perfect for barbecue glazes. Purchase from Middle Eastern food stores, online or at gourmet delicatessens.

SERVES 6 (APPETIZER), 4 (MAIN COURSE) OR 8 (SIDE DISH)

PREPARATION TIME: 1 HOUR

4 tbsp pomegranate molasses

1 tsp ground cinnamon

4 garlic cloves, crushed

salt and freshly ground black pepper

8 boneless quail or skinless, boneless chicken thighs

1 quantity Pomegranate Dressing (see page 150)

200 g/7 oz green beans, trimmed

2 small aubergines (eggplant), cut into 1 cm/½ inch slices

25 g/1 oz/1 cup fresh flat leaf parsley leaves

1 small red onion, finely diced

seeds of 1 pomegranate (optional)

7 tbsp Greek (strained plain) yogurt

Combine the pomegranate molasses, cinnamon and garlic and season with salt and pepper. Rub the mixture all over the quail or chicken thighs, then leave to marinate for at least 30 minutes and up to 3 hours, in the refrigerator.

Pour all dressing ingredients into a screw-top jar, shake well and set aside.

Blanch the green beans in salted, boiling water until al dente, then drain and plunge into iced water. Drain and set aside.

Brush a small amount of the dressing over the aubergine (eggplant) slices and season with salt and pepper.

Heat the barbecue or grill (broiler). Barbecue or grill (broil) the aubergines, then remove and set aside.

Grill the quail or chicken thighs until crispy and golden.

Place the parsley leaves on a large platter. Arrange the beans, aubergines and onion over it and place the quail or chicken on top. Sprinkle with pomegranate seeds and drizzle with the dressing. Place the Greek yogurt in small bowl and serve alongside.

GET ORGANIZED

The dressing and beans could be prepared in the morning. The quail or chicken and aubergines (eggplant) could be cooked 3 hours before eating, but under-cook them and finish the cooking before serving.

VARIATIONS

Loin of lamb could be pan-fried or barbecued and sliced in place of the quail. Couscous or basmati rice would be a good addition to soak up all of the zippy dressing. If you can't obtain pomegranate molasses, substitute 2 tbsp clear honey mixed with 2 tbsp red wine vinegar.

insalata mexicana with goat's cheese,
crab, tortillas and chipotle lime vinaigrette

An irresistible combination of juicy crab meat, crispy lettuce and creamy goat's cheese drizzled in a smoky dressing of lime juice, chipotle chillies and sherry vinegar. Some salty margaritas are required as an accompaniment.

SERVES 6 (APPETIZER), 4 (MAIN COURSE) OR 8 (SIDE DISH)

PREPARATION TIME: 20 MINUTES

4 small handfuls of mesclun, 3 Little Gem (Bibb) or 2 Cos or romaine lettuce hearts

150 g/5 oz goat's cheese, crumbled

250 g/8 oz fresh or drained canned white crab meat

FOR THE VINAIGRETTE

grated rind of 3 limes

1 chipotle chilli in adobo, de-seeded

4 tbsp sherry vinegar

½ tsp ground black pepper

½ tsp salt

125 ml/4 fl oz/½ cup extra virgin olive oil

FOR THE CRISPY TORTILLA STRIPS

4 corn or wheat tortillas, cut into 1 cm/½ inch strips

5 tbsp vegetable oil

Heat the oven to 200°C/400°F/Gas Mark 6.

For the vinaigrette: Place the lime rind, chilli, sherry vinegar, salt and pepper in a food processor and process to a purée. With the machine running, gradually drizzle in the olive oil. Alternatively, you can hand-chop and whisk in a small bowl. Pour into a container and set aside.

For the crispy tortilla strips: Place the tortillas on a baking (cookie) sheet and spray or brush with vegetable oil. Place in the oven for 5 minutes until golden and crispy. Set aside.

Tear the lettuce into 2.5 cm/1 inch pieces and arrange on a platter or individual plates. Sprinkle the goat's cheese and crab over it.

Just before serving, pour the dressing over the salad and top with strips of tortilla.

GET ORGANIZED

The dressing and tortillas can be made the day before. The salad shouldn't be assembled more than 1 hour before serving.

VARIATIONS

Prawns (shrimp), scallops or even shredded pork could be used in place of the crab.

insalata di mare
with radicchio, cherry tomatoes and gremolata

In the Italian port of Amalfi, I devoured an unforgettable seafood salad. The freshest crustaceans were served simply with a squeeze of lemon and drizzle of olive oil. Of course, anytime you try to replicate food from Mediterranean countries, you're in for a challenge. Sometimes a little assistance is required to make up for the dissimilarity in ingredients. Gremolata – a mixture of finely chopped garlic, lemon rind and parsley – is the helping hand in this recipe.

SERVES 6 (APPETIZER), 4 (MAIN COURSE) OR 8 (SIDE DISH)

PREPARATION TIME: 45 MINUTES

8-10 queen scallops, cleaned and trimmed

2 tbsp olive oil

1 tsp salt and freshly ground black pepper

250 g/8 oz large raw prawns (shrimp), peeled and de-veined

500 g/1¼ lb baby squid, cleaned and sliced into 1 cm/½ inch pieces

1 quantity Lemon and Olive Oil Dressing (see page 152)

1 small handful of fresh flat leaf parsley, finely chopped

1 garlic clove, finely chopped

grated rind of 1 lemon

125 g/4 oz red and yellow cherry tomatoes, halved

½ tsp fennel seeds, finely ground

1 radicchio

Drizzle the scallops with a little oil and season with salt and pepper. Heat a grill (broiler) or sauté pan until very hot. Cook the scallops for 1 minute on each side and then place in large bowl.

Bring a large pan of salted water to the boil. Add the prawns (shrimp) and squid. Remove prawns (shrimp) when pink. Boil squid for 3 minutes. Drain and rinse under cold water. Pat dry with tea towels (dishtowels).

Add the prawns and squid to the bowl with the scallops.

Pour all the dressing ingredients into a screw-top jar, shake well and set aside. Combine the parsley, garlic and lemon rind in a small bowl.

Add the tomatoes and fennel seeds to the seafood, pour in the dressing and mix well.

Separate the radicchio into leaves and place them on a large platter. Spoon the seafood on top and sprinkle with the parsley and lemon mixture.

GET ORGANIZED

The dressing can be made the day before and the dressed salad can be prepared 4 hours ahead. However, do not let it sit longer or the seafood will become rubbery.

VARIATIONS

Lobster would be a luxurious addition for a special occasion. Cold orzo noodles (large rice-shaped pasta) would be lovely tossed with the salad. Capers or olives could be added.

lemon grass salmon
with mango and watercress

Even though it was nearly a decade ago when I took a private class at the home of the well-known Asian cook, Sri Owen, the dish we produced has never left my memory – an exotic lemon grass poached salmon served with slices of juicy mango, spicy watercress and a sweet and sour lime dressing.

SERVES 6 (APPETIZER), 4 (MAIN COURSE), 8 (SIDE DISH)

PREPARATION TIME: 40 MINUTES

2 tbsp vegetable oil

1 red onion, thinly sliced

2 garlic cloves, finely chopped

1 small red chilli, de-seeded and finely chopped

2 lemon grass stalks, outer leaves removed and lower third finely chopped

2 inch/5 cm piece of fresh root ginger, finely chopped

2 kaffir lime leaves, finely shredded (optional)

2 tbsp Thai fish sauce

2 tbsp rice vinegar

125 ml/4 fl oz/½ cup hot water

4 salmon fillets, about 100–125 g (3½–4 oz) each

1 quantity Thai Chilli Lime Dressing (see page 153)

1 round (butterhead) lettuce, core removed and leaves separated

2 handfuls of watercress leaves or mizuna

1 mango, peeled, stoned (pitted) and cut into julienne

½ red (bell) pepper, de-seeded and cut into thin julienne

1 small handful of fresh mint leaves

1 small handful of fresh coriander (cilantro) leaves

Heat the oil in a small pan and cook the onion, garlic, chilli, lemon grass and ginger, stirring constantly, for 2 minutes.

Add the lime leaves, Thai fish sauce, vinegar and water and simmer for 4 minutes.

Add the fish and simmer , turning the fish once, for 3-4 minutes. Remove from heat and leave to cool.

Pour all the dressing ingredients into a screw-top jar, shake well and set aside.

Arrange the lettuce leaves and watercress or mizuna on a large platter or individual plates. Place the salmon on them and top with the mango and (bell) pepper slices. Sprinkle with the mint and coriander leaves.

The dressing should be passed separately to each person to pour over the individual salads.

GET ORGANIZED

The salmon can be poached, the vegetables chopped, and the dressing prepared in the morning and stored in the refrigerator.

VARIATIONS

Other firm fish, such as sea bass or halibut, could be used. Lobster or prawns (shrimp) would be good alternatives, too.

lemon crab, fennel and rocket (arugula) salad
with saffron aioli crostini

Crab is so magnificent it doesn't need much adulteration. Here it's tossed with lemon, thin slices of raw fennel and wild rocket (rocket). Alongside is a lusty spoonful of saffron aioli and crispy crostini.

Prepare the aioli and store it in the refrigerator until required. Combine the crab, fennel, chilli and rocket (arugula) in a bowl.

Just before serving, squeeze the lemon and lime juice over the salad, drizzle with the olive oil and season with the salt and pepper. Mix gently and serve on individual plates with the crostini and a spoonful of the aioli.

SERVES 6 (APPETIZER), 4 (MAIN COURSE) OR 8 (SIDE DISH)

PREPARATION TIME: 20 MINUTES

½ quantity Saffron Aioli (see page 150)

500 g/1¼ lb fresh white crab meat

1 fennel bulb, cored and very thinly sliced

1 red chilli, de-seeded and finely chopped

100 g/3½ oz wild rocket (arugula)

juice of ½ lemon

juice of ½ lime

3 tbsp extra virgin olive oil

1 tsp salt

½ tsp fresh cracked black pepper

4 thin slices ciabatta or other Italian bread, toasted

GET ORGANIZED

The aioli can be made the day before and stored in the refrigerator. Everything else should be prepared shortly before serving.

VARIATIONS

Prawns (shrimp) or lobster could be used in place of crab. The salad is excellent without aioli as well.

lamb's lettuce (mâche) with shredded chicken,
wild mushrooms, croûtons and sherry vinegar and walnut oil vinaigrette

Whistling wind, a roaring fire and this salad are all you need for a flawless winter evening. The nutty vinaigrette is absorbed by tender shreds of chicken and crispy croûtons. If you don't feel inclined to roast a whole chicken, buy a cooked one at the supermarket.

SERVES 6 (APPETIZER), 4 (MAIN COURSE) OR 8 (SIDE DISH)

PREPARATION TIME: 1 HOUR 10 MINUTES

1 quantity Sherry Vinegar and Walnut Oil Vinaigrette (see page 60)

1 kg/2¼ lb chicken (organic if possible)

1 tsp sea salt

1 tsp freshly ground black pepper

2 tbsp olive oil

500 g/1¼ lb mixed wild mushrooms, preferably pied de mouton (hedgehog) chestnut, shiitake or chanterelle, trimmed

1 tbsp chopped garlic

4 large handfuls of lamb's lettuce (mâche) or other mild salad leaves (greens), such as baby spinach

1 small handful of flat leaf parsley leaves

100 g/3½ oz, scant 1 cup walnut pieces, toasted

2 small red onions, sliced into thin rings

1 quantity Garlic Croûtons (see page 156)

Heat the oven to 250°C/500°F/Gas Mark 10.

Put all the dressing ingredients in a screw-top jar, shake well and set aside. Place the chicken, breast side down, on a rack in a roasting pan and season with the salt and pepper. Roast for 30 minutes, then turn the chicken over and roast for a further 20–30 minutes or until crispy and brown.

Remove the chicken from the oven and leave to rest for at least 10 minutes. When cool enough, remove the meat, discarding the skin and bones.

Heat the oil in a large sauté pan over a medium high heat. Add the mushrooms and garlic and cook for about 5 minutes until browned. Remove from the pan and set aside in a bowl.

Arrange the lamb's lettuce (mâche) or other salad leaves (greens) on a large platter and shred chicken over it. Add the mushrooms, parsley leaves, walnut pieces, onion rings, and croûtons. Just before serving, pour dressing over the salad.

GET ORGANIZED

The roasted chicken, dressing, croûtons and walnuts can be prepared the day before and stored in an airtight container. Refrigerate the chicken. The salad and mushrooms should be made just before serving the salad.

VARIATIONS

Grilled chicken breasts could be used in place of the whole chicken – use 4 large ones. Goat's cheese or coarsely grated Parmesan would be a lovely addition. Use caramelized walnuts (see page 157) instead of plain toasted ones.

seared raspberry duck,

green bean and spinach salad with caramelized pecans

This duck breast salad is surprisingly easy to make, impressive in appearance, and tantalizingly delicious. The depth of flavour is dramatically improved if you marinate the duck breasts for a couple of hours beforehand.

SERVES 6 (APPETIZER) OR 4 (MAIN COURSE)

PREPARATION TIME: 30 MINUTES, PLUS 2 HOURS FOR MARINATING

4 duck breasts

salt and black pepper

200 g/7 oz baby spinach leaves

150 g/5 oz fine green beans, trimmed

125 g/4 oz cherry tomatoes, halved

1 small red onion, finely diced

1 quantity Raspberry, Balsamic and Nut Oil Vinaigrette (see page 151), made with hazelnut oil

1 quantity Caramelized Nuts (see page 157), made with pecans

FOR THE MARINADE

4 tbsp regular soy sauce

2 tbsp clear honey

4 tbsp raspberry vinegar

1 tbsp balsamic vinegar

2 tbsp walnut or hazelnut oil

salt and black pepper

GET ORGANIZED

The duck breasts can be marinated and the beans, pecans and dressing can be prepared the day before.

VARIATIONS

Sliced beef or lamb fillet would be an excellent alternative to the duck. Figs could replace the beans. Other nuts, such as hazelnuts, could replace pecans. Crumbled goats cheese could be added.

For the marinade. Combine all the marinade ingredients in a shallow, ceramic dish.

Score a criss-cross pattern on the fat side of the duck breasts with knife and season well with salt and pepper. Add to the marinade, turning to coat, and set aside in the refrigerator for at least 2 hours and up to 24 hours.

Heat the oven to 200°C/400°F/Gas Mark 6.

Heat a non-stick sauté pan until very hot. Drain the duck breasts, discard marinade, and pat dry with kitchen paper (paper towels). Sear duck breasts, skin side down. Reduce heat to low and cook for about 10 minutes until the fat has rendered. You want the fat to melt slowly, without burning, so that you have a thin crispy layer of fat.

Transfer the duck to a shallow roasting pan or ovenproof dish and cook in the oven for 10 minutes. Remove from the oven, leave to rest for 10 minutes and then slice thinly.

Arrange the spinach on a platter or individual plates.

Cook the beans in boiling water until al dente, drain and immerse in iced water. Drain again and dry on a tea towel (dishtowel). Arrange the beans on top of the spinach with the tomato and onion.

Place all the vinaigrette ingredients in a screw-top jar, shake well and set aside.

Prepare the caramelized pecans and leave to cool. Sprinkle the pecans over the beans. Place the sliced duck breast on top of each salad.

Just before serving, pour the dressing over the salad and combine well.

tataki of seared tuna
with soy, shallot and ginger dressing

This is a variation of a recipe from the fashionable London restaurant, Nobu. Use only the freshest blue fin tuna, shocking red in colour, with little or no marbling of fat. The recipe works best if you sear the tuna the night before, wrap it tightly and place in the refrigerator. This will make sure that it's firm and easy to cut.

SERVES 6 (APPETIZER), 4 (MAIN COURSE) OR 10 (SIDE DISH)

PREPARATION TIME: 30 MINUTES, PLUS 1 HOUR CHILLING

900 g/2 lb fresh tuna fillet, preferably tail

1 tbsp olive oil

1 tsp salt

2 tsp freshly ground black pepper

30 cm/12 inch piece of mooli (daikon), peeled and cut julienne or 30 cm/ 12 inch piece of cucumber, de-seeded

250 g/8 oz/2 cups spicy salad leaves (greens), such as mizuna, baby red chard, baby mustard, rocket (arugula) or watercress

1 quantity Soy, Shallot and Ginger Dressing (see page 153)

1 tbsp toasted sesame seeds

GET ORGANIZED

Sear the tuna and make the dressing and julienne mooli (daikon) the night before. Soak the mooli in water and store in the refrigerator.

VARIATIONS

Substitute seared prawns (shrimp) or thinly sliced rare beef fillet (tenderloin) for the tuna. You could use tart apples, such as Granny Smith, or jicama, the Mexican vegetable, instead of the mooli. Soba noodles could be used along with the salad leaves (greens).

Cut the tuna lengthways into 2–3 long pieces about 5 cm/2 inches wide that look like small beef fillets (tenderloin).

Heat a large non-stick sauté pan over a medium high heat.

Meanwhile, rub the tuna fillets with the olive oil and then roll them in the salt and pepper, adding more if necessary.

Sear the fillets until brown on all sides, taking care not to overcook as the meat should be rare inside.

Leave to cool slightly, then wrap very tightly in clingfilm (plastic wrap). The tighter it is the easier it will be to slice. Chill for at least 1 hour and preferably up to 12 hours the night before.

Cut the mooli (daikon) or cucumber into fine julienne. For best results, use a mandoline.

Place the prepared salad leaves (greens) on a large platter and pile mooli or cucumber on top.

Unwrap the fish and slice very thinly. Arrange the fish around the sides of the leaves.

Place all the dressing ingredients in a screw-top jar and shake well.

Spoon the dressing over the salad just before serving and sprinkle with the toasted sesame seeds.

Vietnamese prawn (shrimp) salad
with lime, lemon grass and ginger dressing

South-east Asian salads are all about flavour and crunch. Lime, sugar and fish sauce are the magic ingredients that make their dressings exceptional. This one gets an extra burst of taste from lemon grass and ginger. Although it's more time consuming and expensive, buy fresh prawns (shrimp) with their heads and shells on. The taste is miles above that of frozen peeled ones – and yes, the size does matter.

For the dressing: Put the garlic, chillies, lemon grass, shallot and ginger into a food processor and process to a paste. Scrape the paste into a bowl and stir in the Thai fish sauce, sugar, lime juice, coriander (cilantro) and pepper and set aside.

Peel the prawns (shrimp), remove their heads and de-vein with a small paring knife.

Bring a medium pan of water to the boil, add the prawns (shrimp) and remove with a slotted spoon when they turn pink. Rinse prawns under cold water and pat dry on kitchen paper (paper towels).

Combine the carrots, (bell) pepper, cucumbers, red onion, red chilli, mint and the prawns in a large bowl.

Just before serving, pour over the dressing and mix well.

Serve the salad on a large platter with the coriander leaves, spring onions (scallions) and chilli strips sprinkled over it.

SERVES 6 (APPETIZER), 4 (MAIN COURSE) OR 8 (SIDE DISH)

PREPARATION TIME: 30 MINUTES

24 large, raw prawns (shrimp)

2 large carrots, cut into julienne

1 red (bell) pepper, de-seeded and cut into julienne

2 medium cucumbers, de-seeded and thinly sliced

1 red onion, halved and thinly sliced

1 large red chilli, de-seeded and cut into julienne

15 fresh mint leaves

20 g/¾ oz/¾ cup fresh coriander (cilantro) leaves

FOR THE DRESSING

3 garlic cloves, chopped

2 large red chillies, de-seeded and chopped

3 lemon grass stalks, lower third only thinly sliced

1 shallot, thinly sliced

1 tbsp chopped fresh root ginger

3 tbsp Thai fish sauce

4 tbsp sugar

6 tbsp fresh lime juice

½ tsp ground black pepper

FOR THE GARNISH

3 tbsp fresh coriander, chopped

3 spring onions (scallions), white part only cut into julienne and soaked in cold water for 30 minutes

1 large red chilli, de-seeded, cut into julienne and soaked in cold water for 30 minutes

GET ORGANIZED

Peel and poach the prawns (shrimp), chop the vegetables, soak the spring onions (scallions) and make the dressing in the morning.

VARIATIONS

This salad is delicious with chicken, seared beef fillet (tenderloin) or fresh seared tuna in place of prawns. Thin glass (cellophane) or vermicelli noodles could be used for vegetarians. Add crushed peanuts, cashews and/or fried shallots and Fried Ginger Sticks (see page 157).

Thai beef salad

If I had to pick the one salad that I love the most, this would be it. Substantial, bracing and full of zesty flavours, it is a glorious creation.

Marinate the beef in Thai fish sauce and peppercorns for at least 10 minutes and up to 3 hours.

Heat the oven 200°C/400°F/Gas Mark 6.

If using beef fillet (tenderloin), heat a large, heavy pan and sear the meat on each side until browned. Transfer to a roasting pan and roast for 15 minutes until medium rare.

If using sirloin steak, heat a large, heavy pan and sear on both sides until browned. Lower the heat and cook for a little longer until medium rare. It is not necessary to roast.

Leave the beef to rest for 10 minutes before slicing thinly.

Place all the vinaigrette ingredients in a screw-top jar, shake well and set aside.

Combine the tomatoes, cucumbers, onion, beef, lemon grass, mint and coriander (cilantro) in a bowl.

Just before serving, pour the dressing over the salad and combine well. Line a platter with lettuce leaves. Arrange the salad on top of the lettuce and sprinkle with any leftover coriander leaves.

SERVES 6 (APPETIZER), 4 (MAIN COURSE) OR 8 (SIDE DISH)

PREPARATION TIME: 40 MINUTES

1 kg/2¼ lb beef fillet (tenderloin) or sirloin steak

1 tbsp Thai fish sauce

2 tsp crushed black peppercorns

1 quantity Thai Chilli Lime Dressing (see page 153)

500 g/1¼lb ripe cherry tomatoes (preferably pomodorino), halved

8 Lebanese or other small cucumbers, cut into julienne

1 large red onion, thinly sliced

1 lemon grass stalk, thinly sliced (use the lower tender parts only)

handful of fresh mint leaves, chopped

handful of fresh coriander (cilantro) leaves, chopped

20 Cos, romaine or Little Gem (Bibb) lettuce leaves

GET ORGANIZED

All preparation can be done in the morning, but do not add the dressing and onion until just before serving.

VARIATIONS

Adding glass (cellophane) noodles varies the texture. Prawns (shrimp), sliced chicken breast or shredded pork could be used in place of beef. Add some fried shallots or Ginger Sticks (see pages 156-157), or some crushed peanuts. Fry garlic slices in vegetable oil until crispy and scatter over salad.

tandoori prawns (shrimp)
on cucumber and tomato salad

Fat, succulent prawns (shrimp) are marinated in spice-scented yogurt, then pan-grilled and tossed with refreshing cucumbers, tomatoes and a sour lime dressing. An exotic, healthy salad that will have you daydreaming of the shores of Kerala.

SERVES 6 (APPETIZER), 4 (MAIN COURSE) OR 8 (SIDE DISH)

PREPARATION TIME: 30 MINUTES

500 g/1¼ lb large, raw prawns (shrimp), peeled and de-veined

4 tbsp Greek (plain strained) or other full-fat (whole) yogurt

4 tbsp lemon juice

1 tsp paprika

½ tsp ground cumin

2 tsp garam masala or curry powder

1 tsp finely grated fresh root ginger

2 small garlic cloves, crushed

salt and freshly ground black pepper

2 tbsp vegetable oil

4 small Lebanese cucumbers, halved lengthways or 1 large cucumber, halved lengthways and de-seeded

1 small red onion, halved and sliced

250 g/8 oz baby plum or cherry tomatoes, halved

juice of 1 lime

handful of fresh coriander (cilantro) leaves

2 quartered limes, to serve

Pat the prawns (shrimp) thoroughly dry on kitchen paper (paper towels).

Combine the yogurt, lemon juice, paprika, cumin, garam masala or curry powder, ginger garlic, 1 tsp salt, ½ tsp pepper and 1 tbsp of the oil in a medium bowl.

Remove and reserve 125 ml/4 fl oz/ ½ cup of the marinade. Add the prawns to the remaining marinade, coat thoroughly, cover and chill for at least 20 minutes.

Thickly slice the cucumbers or cut into long ribbons with a vegetable peeler. Place them in a bowl with the onion and tomatoes. Squeeze the lime juice over them just before serving and season to taste with salt and pepper.

Heat the remaining oil in non-stick sauté pan over a medium heat. Drain the prawns, add them to the pan and sear until they are browned on both sides.

Arrange the vegetables on a platter and place the prawns on top. Sprinkle coriander (cilantro) leaves over the salad and serve with the lime wedges. Spoon the reserved marinade into a small bowl as additional dressing for the salad. Serve with warm naan or other flat bread.

GET ORGANIZED

The vegetables and marinade can be prepared on the morning of serving. Cook prawns and dress vegetables with lime juice just before serving.

VARIATIONS

Chunks of chicken breasts could be used in place of prawns (shrimp).

side dishes, slaws and potato salads

8

Where would barbecues be without the tasty, crunchy side dishes that make them so exciting? Vinegary potato salads studded with bacon or rainbow-coloured coleslaws in creamy herb dressings are summer on a plate. Potatoes and cabbages have endured a rather unglamorous reputation in the salad world and unjustly so. These undervalued gems thrive with bold tastes and are resilient after hours of being dressed.

Asian savoy cabbage salad

SERVES 6 (APPETIZER),
OR 8 (SIDE DISH)

PREPARATION TIME:
20 MINUTES

½ Savoy cabbage, cored and
thinly sliced

½ red cabbage, thinly sliced

2 carrots, cut into julienne

1 red (bell) pepper, de-seeded
and thinly sliced

1 yellow (bell) pepper,
de-seeded and thinly sliced

8 spring onions (scallions),
thinly sliced

3 shallots, finely chopped

25 g/1 oz/1 cup fresh
coriander (cilantro) leaves

2 tsp salt

1 tsp black pepper

FOR THE DRESSING

juice of 2 limes

1 tbsp regular soy sauce

1½ tbsp finely chopped fresh
ginger root

1 small red chilli, de-seeded
and finely chopped

2 garlic cloves,
finely chopped

1 tbsp clear honey

1 tbsp sesame oil

125 ml/4 fl oz/½ cup
groundnut (peanut) oil

The colour almost beats the taste in this gingery slaw.
Perfect partner for grilled Asian meat.

Put all the vegetables, the coriander (cilantro) and salt and pepper into a large bowl.

Place all the dressing ingredients into a screw-top jar and shake well.

Pour the dressing over the salad and mix well.

VARIATIONS

White cabbage could replace Savoy with great results. Grilled (broiled) prawns (shrimp) or thinly sliced seared beef could be added for a more substantial salad. Crispy Shallots (see page 156) or crushed peanuts would be delicious added.

crunchy cabbage slaw
with creamy cider vinegar dressing

SERVES 6 (APPETIZER),
8 (SIDE DISH)

PREPARATION TIME:
30 MINUTES

250 g/8 oz fennel
bulbs, cored

125 g/4 oz red cabbage

125 g/4 oz green cabbage

1 red (bell) pepper, de-seeded
and finely diced

1 small red onion,
finely chopped

20 g/¾ oz/¾ cup fresh
dill, chopped

20 g/¾ oz/¾ cup fresh flat leaf
parsley, chopped

1 tbsp grated lemon rind

FOR THE DRESSING

2 tbsp sugar

1 tsp Tabasco sauce

5 tbsp mayonnaise

2 tbsp cider vinegar

1 tsp salt

1 tsp freshly ground
black pepper

Classic coleslaw is updated with liquorice-tasting fennel and a tangy creamy dressing.

Use a mandoline or sharp serrated knife to slice the fennel and cabbages as thinly as possible, then coarsely chop the slices. Place in a large bowl.

Add the (bell) pepper, onion, herbs and lemon rind and mix well.

Pour all dressing ingredients into small bowl and whisk until smooth and thoroughly combined.

Mix the dressing with the salad and store in the refrigerator until ready to serve.

three cucumber salads

Highly esteemed for their crisp flesh and refreshing taste, nothing could replace the unique character of cucumbers. They're no upstarts, either, having been around thousands of years. There are endless ways to prepare them, but these are three favourites. Although hothouse specimens are fine, once you've tried Lebanese cucumbers, you'll want to go out of your way to find them. No wider than your thumb, they are sweet, fragrant, have very little water and are worth an extra shopping trip.

SERVES 6 (APPETIZER) OR 8 (SIDE DISH)

PREPARATION TIME: 10 MINUTES FOR EACH RECIPE

FOR CUCUMBER RIBBONS WITH CHILLI, SOY AND GINGER

6 small cucumbers, preferably Lebanese

1 small red chilli, de-seeded and thinly sliced into ribbons

1 tsp finely grated fresh root ginger

2 tbsp soy sauce or sweet soy sauce (kecap manis)

juice of ½ lime

2 tbsp rice wine vinegar

small handful of fresh coriander (cilantro) leaves

FOR SLICED CUCUMBER WITH DILL, RED ONION AND BALSAMIC VINEGAR

6 small cucumbers, preferably Lebanese

15g/½ oz/½ cup fresh dill, finely chopped

½ small red onion, finely chopped

2 tbsp top-quality balsamic vinegar

3 tbsp extra virgin olive oil

½ tsp salt

½ tsp black pepper

FOR CHOPPED CUCUMBERS WITH YOGURT, MINT AND CORIANDER (CILANTRO)

125 ml/4 fl oz/½ cup Greek (plain strained) or other full-fat (whole) yogurt

4 small cucumbers, finely diced, or 1 large cucumber, de-seeded and finely diced

1 small onion, finely diced

2 plum tomatoes, de-seeded and diced

1 garlic clove, crushed

1 tbsp lemon juice

2 tbsp finely chopped fresh mint

1 tbsp finely chopped fresh coriander (cilantro)

½ tsp chilli powder

½ tsp ground cumin

½ tsp each salt and black pepper

For Cucumber Ribbons with Chilli, Soy and Ginger: Using a mandoline, good knife or vegetable peeler, slice the cucumbers into thin slices or thin ribbons. Place them in a medium bowl and toss with all the remaining ingredients just before serving.

For Sliced Cucumber with Dill, Red Onion and Balsamic Vinegar: Cut the cucumbers lengthways and remove seeds with a teaspoon. If using Lebanese, de-seeding is not necessary. Thinly slice the cucumbers and place in a medium bowl. Add all the other ingredients and toss well just before serving.

For Chopped Cucumbers with Yogurt, Mint and Coriander (Cilantro): Place the yogurt in small bowl and beat until creamy. Add all the remaining ingredients and mix well. Serve immediately.

GET ORGANIZED

All dressings could be made on the morning of serving and the salads assembled just before serving.

green papaya salad
with chargrilled beef

The green papaya, a long green fruit sold only in Thai or Asian shops, is an unripe large papaya. Its fabulous texture soaks up lime dressing and absorbs flavours well. Once you've had it, it may become a lifelong addiction.

SERVES 6 (APPETIZER), 4 (MAIN COURSE) OR 8 (SIDE DISH)

PREPARATION TIME: 30 MINUTES

500 g/1¼ lb sirloin steaks, trimmed of fat

1 tbsp Thai fish sauce

1 tbsp groundnut (peanut) or vegetable oil

2 tbsp black peppercorns, crushed

1 quantity Thai Chilli Lime Dressing (see page 153)

1 large green papaya, peeled

4 spring onions (scallions), thinly sliced

1 large cucumber, de-seeded and cut into julienne

25 g/1 oz/1 cup fresh Thai basil leaves or fresh regular basil leaves

20 g/¾ oz/¾ cup fresh mint leaves

20 g/¾ oz/¾ cup fresh coriander (cilantro) leaves

large handful of roasted peanuts or cashew nuts, coarsely chopped

Rub the steaks all over with the fish sauce and oil. Cover both sides with peppercorns.

Heat a medium pan until it is very hot. Sear both sides of the steaks for about 3 minutes on each side. Leave to rest for 5–10 minutes, then slice very thinly and set aside.

Put all the dressing ingredients into a screw-top jar, shake well and set aside.

Cut the green papaya into thin julienne using a knife or mandoline. Alternatively, use the coarse side of a grater. In this case, place a bowl in the sink and hold the grater on the side of work surface (counter) above it. Using a long movement, grate the side of the papaya to produce long, elegant pieces. Be careful not to slice or grate past the soft part in the middle where the seeds are. Once you get close to the seeds, discard the papaya. It is important that the julienne are long, as they add to the texture of the salad, so do not grate into short pieces.

Add the spring onions (scallions), sliced steak, cucumber, basil, mint, coriander (cilantro) and dressing to the green papaya. Toss well, taste and add more Thai fish sauce or lime juice, if necessary.

Just before serving, add the chopped peanuts or cashew nuts.

GET ORGANIZED

The dressing, spring onions (scallions), beef and green papaya can be prepared in morning. The cucumber should be sliced no earlier than 1 hour before serving or it will become watery. Once the salad has been assembled, it should be served within 1 hour.

VARIATIONS

The salad can be served plain with no meat. Green beans and tomatoes quarters can be added. Prawns, chicken or pork can replace the beef. Crispy Shallots (see page 156) would be lovely sprinkled on top.

Italian potato salad with red onion,
pancetta, parsley and red wine vinaigrette

SERVES 6 (APPETIZER),
4 (MAIN COURSE) OR
8 (SIDE DISH)

PREPARATION TIME:
30 MINUTES

500 g/1¼ lb small red potatoes

2 tsp salt

½ quantity Classic Red Wine
Vinaigrette (see page 150)

250 g/8 oz/1½ cups cubed or
streaky slices of pancetta

1 red onion, finely chopped

large bunch of fresh flat leaf
parsley, finely chopped

1 tsp freshly ground
black pepper

My mother used to make this favourite when I was growing up, and it's equally good served hot or cold. The potatoes soak up the vinaigrette and other seasonings while steaming hot. Be sure to use red potatoes to achieve the creamy texture.

Cook the potatoes in a pan of boiling water with 1 tsp salt until they are easily pierced with the point of a knife. Drain, return to the pan and leave to dry.

Put all the vinaigrette ingredients into a screw-top jar, shake well and set aside.

Fry the pancetta in a small sauté pan until very crisp, then drain on kitchen paper (paper towels).

Slice the potatoes into 1 cm/½ inch thick pieces and place in large bowl. Add the pancetta, onion, parsley, the remaining salt, the pepper and vinaigrette. Mix gently, taste and add more salt or vinegar, if necessary.

GET ORGANIZED

The entire salad can be prepared the day before and stored in the refrigerator.

VARIATIONS

Chopped fresh basil, mint or chives can replace or be added to the parsley. Chopped olives or capers would work well.

potato salad
with crème fraîche, dill and red onion

SERVES 6 (APPETIZER)
OR 8 (SIDE DISH)

PREPARATION TIME:
30 MINUTES

500 g/1¼ lb small red potatoes

2 tsp salt

4 tbsp cider vinegar

250 ml/8 fl oz/1 cup crème
fraîche or sour cream

20 g/¾ oz/¾ cup fresh dill,
finely chopped

1 red onion, finely chopped

1 head of celery hearts,
thinly sliced

1 tbsp rinsed capers

1 tsp black pepper

Delicate red potatoes are doused in a robust dressing of crème fraîche and dill while they are still warm. A lovely summer indulgence alongside salmon or other fish.

Cook the potatoes in a pan of boiling water with 1 tsp salt until they are easily pierced with the point of a knife. Drain, return to the pan and leave to dry.

When the potatoes are cool enough to handle, cut them into 1 cm/½ inch slices and place in large bowl.

Drizzle with cider vinegar, sprinkle with the remaining salt and mix gently. Add the crème fraîche or sour cream, onion, celery, dill, capers and pepper and mix well. Store in the refrigerator until ready to serve.

VARIATIONS

Thin slices of smoked salmon could be added. Omit the crème fraîche or sour cream and use a dressing such as like Sherry Vinegar and Walnut Oil Vinaigrette (see page 60), Classic Red Wine Vinaigrette (see page 150) or Balsamic Dressing (see page 150).

juicy fruit

9

Fruit bursts with vibrant colours,
and sweet lusciousness. That is,
of course, if it is ripe and in
season. Put your nose against any
mango, peach or melon and smell
its intense fragrance. It's juicy
composition partners well with
savoury ingredients and more
composing is required than cooking.
Sugary pineapple, dramatic red blood oranges
or dark purple figs are just a few of the rich
selection that make memorable salads.

avocado, orange and red onion salad
with black olive vinaigrette

SERVES 6 (APPETIZER),
4 (MAIN COURSE) OR
8 (SIDE DISH)

PREPARATION TIME:
15 MINUTES

large handful of rocket
(arugula) leaves (optional)

2 avocados, peeled and
stoned (pitted)

2 oranges (preferably navel
or blood varieties)

1 small red onion,
thinly sliced

15g/ ½ oz/½ cup fresh basil
leaves or flat leaf parsley,
coarsely chopped

**FOR THE BLACK
OLIVE VINAIGRETTE**

2 tbsp chopped pitted
black olives

2 tbsp sherry or red
wine vinegar

4 tbsp extra virgin olive oil

½ shallot, finely chopped

½ tsp salt

½ tsp ground black pepper

These ingredients have a special affinity for one other. Not only does this salad feature vibrant colour, its taste is uplifting and it is ultra simple to prepare.

Place a little rocket (arugula) on each serving plate or on a large platter.

Thinly slice the avocados and arrange the slices on top.

Using a sharp knife, cut the peel and pith off the oranges, remove any pips (seeds) and then cut the flesh into 1 cm/½ inch slices. Cut each slice into quarters and arrange on top of the avocado.

Sprinkle the red onion slices and basil or parsley over the salad.

Put all the vinaigrette ingredients into a screw-top jar and shake well. Pour the dressing over salad and serve immediately.

GET ORGANIZED

The salad should be eaten fairly soon after it has been prepared. If you want to make it 1 hour before, squeeze fresh lemon or lime juice over the avocados and do not add the onion until just before serving. The vinaigrette can be made the day before and refrigerated.

avocado and hearts of palm salad

SERVES 6 (APPETIZER)
OR 8 (SIDE DISH)

PREPARATION TIME:
10 MINUTES

2 ripe Haas avocados, peeled
and stoned (pitted)

200g/7 oz can palm
hearts, drained

1 small red onion,
finely diced

1 tsp extra virgin olive oil

2 tsp red wine vinegar

1 tsp each salt and
black pepper

60 g/2 oz Parmesan cheese,
thinly shaved

Palm hearts are a Brazilian ingredient harvested from palm trees. Slender and ivory coloured, they taste a little like artichokes. Most supermarkets stock them alongside other water-packed canned vegetables. You'll soon find yourself putting them in everything. They are very handy for whipping up quick appetizers when there's not much in the refrigerator.

Cut the avocados and palm hearts into 1 cm/½ inch pieces and place in a bowl with the red onion.

Sprinkle with the olive oil, vinegar, salt and pepper.

Divide the salad evenly among 4 or 8 plates and garnish with Parmesan shavings. Serve immediately.

GET ORGANIZED

The salad should be served straight after preparation to keep the avocados from going brown. Otherwise, squeeze lemon juice over it to prevent discoloration for a maximum of 1 hour.

VARIATIONS

Slices of tomatoes or mozzarella cheese go well with this salad. Chunks of crab or crispy fried bacon would be tasty additions.

blood orange, fennel, potato and parsley salad
with sherry vinaigrette

SERVES 6 (APPETIZER),
4 (MAIN COURSE) OR
8 (SIDE DISH)

PREPARATION TIME:
20 MINUTES

4 medium-sized red-skinned potatoes, boiled and peeled

2 fennel bulbs, cored, and thinly sliced

1 small red onion, thinly sliced

4 blood or navel oranges

small handful of fresh flat leaf parsley leaves

2 tbsp sherry vinegar

4 tbsp extra virgin olive oil

½ tsp sea salt

½ tsp freshly ground black pepper

Surprisingly, oranges are ideally paired with potatoes – the clean, assertive citrus juice cutting the starch to provide a perfect balance.

Cut the potatoes into 1 cm/½ inch thick slices and place them on large platter. Arrange the fennel and onion slices over them.

Using a sharp knife, cut peel and pith away from oranges. Cut the flesh into 1 cm/½ inch slices and remove any pips (seeds). Place oranges over the other vegetables on the platter and sprinkle with parsley.

Drizzle sherry vinegar and olive oil over the salad, sprinkle with the salt and pepper and serve.

GET ORGANIZED

The salad is best made within 1 hour of serving to keep the ingredients at their freshest.

VARIATIONS

Black olives, pomegranate seeds or chopped pistachios would be an attractive addition. Serrano ham, proscuitto, or thinly sliced chorizo would all make tasty additions.

mesclun and raspberry salad

with parmesan tuiles and raspberry, balsamic and walnut oil vinaigrette

A delicate salad bursting with colour, texture and harmonious flavours. The Parmesan tuiles look impressive and are straightforward to make. You must use non-stick baking parchment to make sure that they are easy to remove.

SERVES 6 (APPETIZER), 4 (MAIN COURSE) OR 8 (SIDE DISH)

PREPARATION TIME: 30 MINUTES

4 large handfuls of mesclun (mixed baby lettuces)

200 g/7 oz raspberries

4 spring onions (scallions), white part only thinly sliced

1 quantity Raspberry, Balsamic and Nut Oil Vinaigrette (see page 151), made with walnut oil

1 quantity Parmesan Tuiles

1 quantity Caramelized walnuts or 60 g/2 oz/ ½ cup toasted walnuts

small handful of fresh flat leaf parsley leaves

Place the mesclun on individual plates or a large platter and arrange the raspberries, parsley and spring onions (scallions) on top.

Pour all the vinaigrette ingredients into a screw-top jar, shake well and set aside.

Prepare the parmesan tuiles and caramelized walnuts, if using, and leave to cool,

Arrange the tuiles and caramelized or toasted walnuts over the salad and just before serving, drizzle with the dressing.

GET ORGANIZED

The dressing, Parmesan tuiles and caramelized walnuts can be prepared the day before and stored in an airtight container. The spring onions (scallions) should be added to the salad until just before serving.

VARIATIONS

Use chunks of Gorgonzola or goat's cheese instead of Parmesan tuiles. Slices of prosciutto, rare beef fillet (tenderloin), grilled chicken, duck breast or pan-fried chicken livers would suit the salad well.

figs, mozzarella, basil and prosciutto
with balsamic vinegar

The best type of figs to use are purple-black Missions, so named because they were introduced to California by Spanish missionaries. These figs have luscious sweet red centres and very small seeds. Other varieties, imported from Turkey and the Middle East, are in season from June to October. Remember to keep your mozzarella at room temperature, as chilling alters the cheese's texture. Only top-quality vinegars and oils will do here.

Drape 2 slices of prosciutto over each of 4 plates or drape all the slices on a large platter. Place 8 fig quarters on each plate.

Rip each mozzarella ball into 5 cm/2 inch chunks and divide among the plates. Sprinkle the basil leaves over each plate.

Just before serving, drizzle balsamic vinegar and olive oil over the salads and sprinkle with the salt and pepper. Serve immediately.

SERVES 6 (APPETIZER), 4 (MAIN COURSE) OR 8 (SIDE DISH)

PREPARATION TIME: 10 MINUTES

8 slices of prosciutto

8 ripe figs, quartered

4 buffalo mozzarella balls, drained

large handful of fresh basil leaves, torn in half

4 tbsp 10-year aged or other good-quality balsamic vinegar

4 tbsp extra virgin olive oil

1 tsp salt

1 tsp freshly ground black pepper

GET ORGANIZED

The ingredients can be prepared on the day, but not assembled together until just before serving or the mozzarella will make everything milky.

VARIATIONS

Dried figs plumped up in warm balsamic vinegar or saba would be tremendous in the winter months. Rocket (arugula) or mesclun could be added. Sprinkle chopped pistachios over.

prawn (shrimp), pork and pineapple salad
with thai chilli lime dressing and fried ginger sticks

"Pork, prawns (shrimp) and pineapple", you say? Hmmm… Stay with me, because this classic Thai salad is a fantastic combination. Sweet pineapple, tender minced (ground) pork and succulent large prawns are imbued with a spicy lime dressing and crunchy ginger. Take a walk on the wild side with this exotic dish.

SERVES 6 (APPETIZER), 4 (MAIN COURSE) OR 8 (SIDE DISH)

PREPARATION TIME: 30 MINUTES

250 g/8 oz large raw prawns (shrimp), peeled

1 tbsp vegetable oil

250 g/8 oz minced (ground) pork

1 red (bell) pepper, de-seeded and finely diced

1 red onion, finely diced

1 ripe pineapple, peeled, cored and sliced into 1 cm/½ inch pieces

15 g/½ oz/½ cup fresh mint leaves, finely chopped

15 g/½ oz/½ cup fresh basil leaves, finely chopped

1 quantity Fried Ginger Sticks (see page 157)

1 quantity Thai Chilli Lime Dressing (see page 153)

2 Little Gem (Bibb) lettuces, leaves separated

small handful of fresh coriander (cilantro) leaves, to garnish

Cook the prawns (shrimp) in boiling water until they turn pink. Drain and immediately immerse in iced water. Drain again and pat dry on kitchen paper (paper towels).

Heat the oil in a sauté pan. Add the pork and cook until browned, breaking it up with a spoon. Leave to cool slightly, then place in bowl with the prawns, red (bell) pepper, onion, pineapple, mint and basil.

Prepare the ginger sticks and set aside.

Pour all the dressing ingredients into a screw-top jar and shake well. Alternatively, you can use a mortar and pestle and pound the dry ingredients to a paste, adding the fish sauce and lime juice last. Pour the dressing over the salad and mix gently.

Arrange the lettuce leaves on a large platter and spoon the salad over them. Sprinkle with the coriander (cilantro) leaves and serve immediately.

GET ORGANIZED

All the ingredients and the dressing can be prepared on the day, but should not be assembled until just before serving.

VARIATIONS

Crab or lobster could be used in place of prawns (shrimp). Julienne of carrot could be included as an additional vegetable. Crispy fried shallots (see page 156) or garlic could replace the ginger sticks.

prosciutto-wrapped melon and rocket (arugula)
with balsamic vinegar

This dish is more about arranging superb ingredients than about cooking them. Ripe melon and top-quality oil and vinegar are essential for this quintessential summer salad.

Arrange the rocket (arugula) on individual plates or a large platter.

Wrap each piece of melon with a slice of prosciutto and place on top of the rocket.

Just before serving, drizzle with the oil and vinegar and sprinkle with the pistachios and salt and pepper. Serve immediately.

SERVES 6 (APPETIZER), 4 (MAIN COURSE) OR 8 (SIDE DISH)

PREPARATION TIME: 10 MINUTES

2 large handfuls of rocket (arugula)

1 ripe cantaloupe or honeydew melon, peeled, seeded and cut into 8 slices

8 slices of prosciutto

4 tbsp extra virgin olive oil

4 tbsp 10-year old balsamic vinegar

½ tsp sea salt

½ tsp freshly ground black pepper

60 g/2 oz pistachio nuts, chopped

GET ORGANIZED

Everything should be done just before serving to keep the salad from becoming soggy.

VARIATIONS

Other ripe seasonal fruit, such as peaches, could be used instead of melon. Shaved Parmesan cheese would be a delicious addition.

goat's cheese stuffed figs
wrapped in bacon on rocket (arugula)

Warm figs stuffed with oozing goat's cheese, crispy bacon and a sweet balsamic dressing makes for an enticing winter salad. Use purple Mission or Turkish figs; green varieties aren't so tasty.

SERVES 6 (APPETIZER), 4 (MAIN COURSE) OR 8 (SIDE DISH)

PREPARATION TIME: 45 MINUTES

16 slices (strips) of thin streaky bacon

8 fresh ripe figs, still firm

125 g/4 oz hard or semi-hard goat's cheese, cut into 8 pieces

2 tbsp brown sugar

1 tsp each salt and black pepper

2 large handfuls of rocket (arugula) or mesclun

1 quantity Balsamic Dressing (see page 152)

Heat the grill (broiler).

Cook the bacon in a large sauté pan until it is tender and has rendered most of its fat. Drain on kitchen paper (paper towels).

Cut each fig almost into quarters without cutting completely through. Using a small melon baller, scoop out 1 ball from the centre of each fig.

Fill each fig with 1 piece of goat's cheese, then press the quarters together to re-form a whole fig.

Wrap 2 bacon slices around each fig and secure with a wooden cocktail stick (toothpick).

Mix together the sugar, salt, pepper and brown sugar and rub each bacon-wrapped fig with the mixture.

Pour all the dressing ingredients into a screw-top jar, shake well and set aside.

Divide the rocket (arugula) among individual plates.

Arrange the figs on a baking (cookie) sheet and grill (broil) for about 3 minutes until brown.

Place the figs on the rocket and pour the dressing over them just before serving.

GET ORGANIZED

The dressing can be made the day before. The figs can be prepared with the goat's cheese and bacon in the morning and stored in the refrigerator. Rub with the sugar mixture just before cooking.

VARIATIONS

Tallegio cheese or Gorgonzola could be used in place of goat's cheese. Caramelized Nuts (see page 157) could be added.

sea bass ceviche
with mango, red onion and coriander (cilantro)

Paper-thin slices of sea bass are "cooked" in lime juice and paired with juicy mango, red onion and crunchy pieces of corn tortillas. It goes without saying that you should purchase only the highest quality, freshest possible fish for this. Home-made margaritas or caipirinhas are the compulsory cocktails to accompany.

Arrange the sea bass slices in a flat serving dish. Pour half the lime juice over them and set aside in the refrigerator for 30 minutes or until the fish has turned opaque.

Heat the oil in small, heavy pan and line a bowl with kitchen paper (paper towels). Check the temperature of the oil with a small piece of tortilla; if it is hot enough, the tortilla will crisp and bubble very quickly. When the oil is hot, add the tortilla chips and cook for 30 seconds, until crisp. Remove with a slotted spoon and drain in the prepared bowl. Alternatively, spray the tortilla pieces with oil and bake in a preheated oven at 200°C/400°F/Gas Mark 6 for 8 minutes.

Remove the fish from the lime juice and place in a bowl. Add the mango, chopped coriander (cilantro), onion and chilli.

Just before serving, add the remaining lime juice and season with the salt and pepper. Serve on individual plates, garnished with coriander and with the tortilla chips on the side.

SERVES 6 (APPETIZER) OR 4 (MAIN COURSE)

PREPARATION TIME: 15 MINUTES, PLUS 30 MINUTES FOR MARINATING

500 g/1¼ lb sea bass fillet, skinned and very thinly sliced

250 ml/8 fl oz/1 cup fresh lime juice

250 ml/8 fl oz/1 cup vegetable or groundnut (peanut) oil

4 corn tortillas, cut into 3 pieces each

1 large ripe mango, peeled, stoned (pitted) and very thinly sliced

small handful of fresh coriander (cilantro), leaves, coarsely chopped

1 small red onion, finely chopped

1 small fresh red chilli, de-seeded and chopped or 1 chipotle chilli in adobo sauce, finely chopped

½ tsp salt

½ tsp freshly ground black pepper

fresh coriander leaves, to garnish

GET ORGANIZED

The sea bass shouldn't be marinated for more than 1 hour before serving or it will become rubbery. The lime dressing should be poured over just before serving or the mangoes will become mushy.

VARIATIONS

Swordfish or tuna could be used instead of sea bass. If you don't want to go to the trouble of making tortillas chips, simply substitute crisp leaves of Cos or romaine hearts. You can also finely dice the fish and mangoes and serve as a dip or canapé.

must-have dressings and vinaigrettes

A salad is not complete without the finishing touches. Whatever dressing you want, the method is, almost without exception, the same – pour the ingredients into a screw-top jar and shake. There isn't a set formula for ratios of vinegar to oil, it depends on individual taste. Adjust the recipes according to whether you prefer a milder flavour or to pucker your lips. Invest in superb vinegars and oils. An over-acidic cheap vinegar can make or break a salad, so look for high-quality, aged products. Mix and match these vinaigrettes with any of the recipes in the book.

CLASSIC RED WINE VINAIGRETTE

Light and tasty for mild salad leaves (greens), but this versatile dressing could be used on almost any salad.

4 tbsp red wine vinegar

7 tbsp extra virgin olive oil

1 garlic clove, finely chopped

½ tsp Dijon mustard

1 tsp sugar

½ tsp each salt and freshly ground black pepper

ANCHOVY, CAPER AND GARLIC DRESSING

This makes Greek salad taste like a dream and is excellent over mozzarella or fried halloumi cheese.

1 anchovy packed in oil, rinsed and chopped

10 small capers, rinsed and chopped

1 garlic clove, finely chopped

½ tsp salt

½ tsp freshly ground black pepper

125 ml/4 fl oz/½ cup good quality red wine vinegar (Cabernet Sauvignon)

7 tbsp extra virgin olive oil

POMEGRANATE DRESSING

Sweet, sour and exotic, this is one of the best for North African or Mediterranean salads.

5 tbsp pomegranate molasses

juice of ½ lemon

1 garlic clove, crushed

½ tsp ground cumin

1 tsp sugar

5 tbsp extra virgin olive oil

½ tsp each salt and freshly ground black pepper

SWEET AND SPICY VINAIGRETTE

This works well with pasta and fresh salad greens.

1 tbsp sherry vinegar

1 tbsp cassis, fig or balsamic vinegar

2 tbsp Classic Red Wine Vinaigrette (see above)

125 ml/4 fl oz/½ cup extra virgin olive oil

1 tsp Dijon mustard

1 garlic clove, finely chopped

1 tsp sugar

½ tsp crushed red chillies

1 tsp salt

½ tsp black pepper

CITRUS CAPER DRESSING

Use this piquant dressing for mozzarella cheese, aubergines (eggplant) or lentils.

2 tbsp capers, rinsed and chopped

1 garlic clove, finely chopped

½ shallot, finely chopped

3 tbsp finely chopped fresh flat leaf parsley

1 tbsp grainy French mustard

1 tbsp orange juice

2 tbsp red wine vinegar

3 tbsp extra virgin olive oil

½ tsp each salt and black pepper

SHERRY AND OLIVE OIL VINAIGRETTE

This dressing complements bitter salad leaves (greens), such as chicory (Belgian endive) and watercress, but is equally good on lentils and beans.

3 tbsp sherry vinegar

6 tbsp extra virgin olive oil

½ tsp Dijon mustard

1 tsp sugar

½ tsp salt

½ tsp freshly ground black pepper

SAFFRON AIOLI

This garlic-flavoured mayonnaise is superb for potato salad or Provençal pan-grilled vegetables.

2 egg yolks, at room temperature

1 tsp saffron threads, soaked in 2 tbsp hot water

4 garlic cloves, finely chopped

½ tsp each salt and black pepper

250 ml/8 fl oz/1 cup equal parts olive oil and groundnut (peanut) oil

juice of ½ lemon

Place the egg yolks, saffron and soaking water, garlic and salt and pepper in a food processor or blender and process briefly to combine.

With the machine running, gradually add the oil in until the mixture is thick and emulsified.

Add the lemon juice and pulse once more. Alternatively, you can use a small bowl and whisk.

If your aioli doesn't thicken, scrape it out of the food processor into a jug (pitcher). Put 1 tbsp prepared mayonnaise into the food processor and switch on. Gradually drizzle in the aioli mixture in until it is emulsified.

RASPBERRY BALSAMIC AND NUT OIL VINAIGRETTE

Excellent for mesclun or spinach salads, whichever type of nut oil you choose.

4 tbsp raspberry vinegar

2 tbsp balsamic vinegar

4 tbsp olive oil

3 tbsp hazelnut or walnut oil

1 tsp Dijon mustard

½ tsp each salt and freshly ground black pepper

TAMARIND AND LEMON GRASS DRESSING

Use this punchy dressing for noodles, Asian slaws or Thai salads.

100 g/3½ oz jar prepared tamarind liquid

4 tbsp water

2 tbsp vegetable oil

juice of 2 limes

1½ tbsp regular soy sauce

2 tbsp clear honey

1 tbsp grated fresh root ginger

(continued below)

GRAINY MUSTARD VINAIGRETTE

A hearty dressing for lentils, potatoes, coleslaw or Cos or romaine lettuce.

1 garlic clove, finely chopped

125 ml/4 fl oz/½ cup extra virgin olive oil

2 tbsp red wine vinegar

1 tbsp balsamic vinegar

1 tbsp grainy mustard

1 tsp salt

½ tsp freshly ground black pepper

1 garlic clove

1 fresh red chilli, de-seeded

2 lemon grass stalks, outer leaves and top 3 inches discarded

½ tsp black pepper

Place all ingredients in food processor and pulse until smooth. Alternatively, you can chop everything by hand and mix in small bowl.

HARISSA DRESSING

Use this delicious North African dressing on carrots, couscous or roasted vegetables.

125 ml/4 fl oz/½ cup extra virgin olive oil

2 tsp harissa paste

1 garlic clove, crushed

½ tsp ground cumin

juice of 1 lemon

1 tsp chopped fresh mint

1 tsp chopped fresh parsley

1 tsp salt

1 tsp clear honey

½ tsp black pepper

SWEET SOY, GINGER AND CHILLI DRESSING

Made sweet and thick with kecap manis, an Indonesian soy sauce, use as dressing or dipping sauce.

5 tbsp sweet soy sauce (kecap manis) or 5 tbsp dark soy sauce mixed with 1 tbsp brown sugar

2 thumb-sized red chillies, de-seeded and chopped

3 garlic cloves, finely chopped

1 tbsp finely chopped fresh root ginger

(continued below)

LEMON AND OLIVE OIL DRESSING

Lovely and simple, this dressing is perfect for Mediterranean and leafy salads.

juice of 1 lemon

½ tsp grated lemon rind

5 tbsp extra virgin olive oil

1 tbsp clear honey

½ tsp each salt and freshly ground black pepper

BALSAMIC DRESSING

This classic sweet dressing complements almost any salad.

5 tbsp good-quality balsamic vinegar

125 ml/4 fl oz/½ cup extra virgin olive oil

1 garlic clove, finely chopped

1 tsp Dijon mustard

1 tsp sugar

1 tsp salt

½ tsp freshly ground black pepper

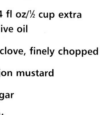

juice of 2 limes

1 tbsp rice vinegar

2 tbsp sugar

½ tsp black pepper

Mix all the ingredients in a small bowl. Alternatively, put everything into a food processor and pulse until smooth.

ROASTED TOMATO, OLIVE AND RED ONION DRESSING

This pairs well with beans, pasta and lentils.

6 Oven-dried Cherry Tomatoes (see page 156), chopped

4 black olives, pitted and finely chopped

1 small red onion, finely chopped

1 small bunch of fresh basil, finely chopped

7 tbsp balsamic or red wine vinegar

125 ml/4 fl oz/½ cup extra virgin olive oil

½ tsp each salt and freshly ground black pepper

ROASTED GARLIC AND HERB DRESSING

The gutsy flavours perk up otherwise plain ingredients such as lentils and beans.

8 garlic cloves, unpeeled

1 tsp Dijon mustard

2 tbsp chopped fresh parsley

2 tbsp red wine vinegar

1 tbsp sherry vinegar

1 tbsp balsamic vinegar

125 ml/4 fl oz/½ cup extra virgin olive oil

(continued below)

SOY, SHALLOT AND GINGER DRESSING

This is just gorgeous on spicy leaves (greens), noodles, chicken or seared tuna.

2 tbsp finely chopped shallot

3 tbsp regular soy sauce

2½ tbsp rice vinegar

2 tsp water

½ tsp sugar

1 tsp grated fresh root ginger

4 tsp vegetable oil

4 tsp sesame oil

½ tsp freshly ground black pepper

THAI CHILLI LIME DRESSING

This sweet, sour, salty and spicy dressing used on south-east Asian salads pairs well with noodles, chicken, beef or prawns (shrimp).

125 ml/4 fl oz/½ cup fresh lime juice

2 tsp sugar

1 garlic clove, crushed

½ medium red chilli, de-seeded and chopped

2 tbsp Thai fish sauce

1 tbsp chopped fresh coriander (cilantro)

1 tsp clear honey

½ tsp each salt and freshly ground black pepper

Place the garlic cloves in a dry pan. Blacken on both sides, cool and then peel. Chop coarsely. Add to remaining ingredients and shake in a screw-top jar.

MISO GINGER DRESSING

Lovely for tomatoes, vegetables and Japanese-inspired salads.

3 tbsp miso paste

1 garlic clove, finely chopped

3 tbsp mirin

1 tbsp sugar

1 tsp grated lemon rind

1 tbsp sesame oil

1 tbsp Japanese soy sauce

1 tbsp grated fresh root ginger

4 tbsp rice wine vinegar

5 tbsp vegetable oil

½ tsp black pepper

salt, to taste

the sweet and sour
oils and vinegars

Creating a memorable salad is not difficult if you're armed with the right vinegars and oils. Even humble lettuce becomes aristocratic when adorned with a few drops of walnut oil and top-quality sherry vinegar. Avoid bland oils and cheap, throat-catching vinegars; they can sabotage choice ingredients and hard work. Instead, focus on brands with proper ageing, sharp flavours, and good colour. Whether you use the classics or venture into the new genre of exciting oils and vinegars, you need only to focus on taste and quality!

VINEGARS

Balsamic – made from the white Trebbiano grape, this aged wine vinegar is intensely dark, powerfully aromatic and tastes both sweet and tart. It is sold commercially and as *aceto balsamico tradizionale*. The traditional ages in casks for minimum of 12 years, making it expensive, exquisite and a requirement for salad making. It is best used for drizzling, rather than large quantities of dressing. Factory-made brands aren't given the same loving care, so they lack depth, but are still tasty. Italian or Mediterranean salads suit it best.

White balsamic – Made by an entirely different process from real balsamic vinegar, this is produced by combining Champagne vinegar with concentrated grape juice for a sweet white wine vinegar. It is lovely in mild dressings for baby lettuces.

Cider vinegar – This hearty, golden-coloured vinegar is made from apples. Its fruity and tart nature works well in mayonnaise dressings, potato salads and coleslaws.

Champagne vinegar – A wine vinegar made from Champagne stock, before the bubbles in the second fermentation. With a delicate character and a clean taste, it is well suited to light vinaigrettes for vegetables and lettuces.

Rice vinegar – Both Japanese and Chinese vinegars are made from fermented white rice. It is delicate, with a pale clear colour and a mild sweet and sour flavour. Brown rice vinegar is another variation. Pale amber in colour and made from brown rice, it has slightly more depth than the white. Rice vinegar is best used in Asian slaws, noodles and aubergine (eggplant) salads.

Sherry vinegar – Spanish vinegar, made from sweet Oloroso sherry, is aged at least 10 years in oak casks until it is transformed into a complex, full-bodied vinegar. Raisin-like, smoky and nutty, it has an intense flavour that is particularly complementary to North African, Mexican and Spanish cuisine. Look for quality brands with the ageing listed on the label.

Wine vinegar – Made from red or white wine, this is the most frequently found vinegar. Depending on the maker, the colour, acidity and flavour vary dramatically. White should be used in a similar way to Champagne vinegar. Particularly notable is the Chardonnay white, which has a sweet, subtle taste. The best reds are made using the Orléans process in which high-quality wine ferments in barrels for months. Italian, French and Spanish producers export the best quality. Look for the ruby-coloured Cabernet Sauvignon or Chianti, which are intensely flavoured and low in acidity.

Flavoured vinegars – Made by infusing herbs or chillies into white wine vinegar, it has a clean acidic flavour and herbaceous taste. Most are sold for decorative rather than culinary purposes. Tarragon vinegar is an exception, lending a tangy taste to pasta or rice salads. Quality can vary, so look carefully at the producer to avoid over-acidic brands. French imports are very good.

Fruit vinegars – The method for producing these varies from macerating fruit in white wine or Champagne vinegar to mixing purées with vinegar. France is reputed for its raspberry, but there are many others available, such as pear, blueberry, pineapple and mango. Cassis balsamic vinegar is slightly different, combining red wine vinegar with blackcurrant concentrate. Fruit vinegars are best used with nut oils for delicate mesclun or salads involving fruit.

Black vinegar – A black-coloured vinegar made by the Chinese. It has a smoky, sweet flavour and is made from black rice or millet. It can be difficult to find, unless you shop in an Asian food market, so substitute with a light, inexpensive balsamic vinegar. Its unique taste compliments noodles and soy-based dressings.

Walnut and hazelnut oils – Aromatic and elegant, these oils are cold-pressed, which preserves their nutty taste. Unfortunately, they lose their fragrance quickly and need to be used within 3 months of opening. It is best to store them in a cool, dark place after opening. They are magnificent mixed with fruit or sherry vinegars for frisée or mesclun salads.

Groundnut (peanut oil) – Most groundnut oil is not cold pressed and therefore has little or no flavour. You can find cold-pressed with a true nutty taste at Asian markets. It is more expensive than vegetable oils and is respected for its high smoke point and lack of odour while frying. The Asian variety is particularly good in soy based dressings.

Sesame oil – Olive and sesame are the oldest oils in history, going back to the ancient Egyptians. Extracted from toasted sesame seeds, this dark oil has a nutty aroma. Most Asians use it for flavour accent. Excellent in s oy-based dressings for noodles, aubergines (eggplant) or poultry.

Pumpkin oil – A thick, robust oil made from roasted pumpkin seeds, it is dark green in colour. Because of its strong nature, it is best drizzled alone over grilled vegetables or mixed with other oils for dressings.

OILS

Olive oil – Olive oil making is an ancient technique going back to 3000 BC. "Extra virgin olive oil" is the first pressing of ripe olives and yields the finest quality. Subsequent pressings are labelled "virgin olive oil", then "pure olive oil" and quality diminishes with each extraction. Unless I'm making a mayonnaise, I don't recommend using so-called pure olive oil, as it doesn't offer much aroma. Extra virgin has a greeny-gold colour and a fruity to peppery flavour, which varies depending on the country and producer. It's a personal taste as to which country's oil you like best; but I rate Tuscan as the finest, with other Italian regions close behind. Spanish and Greek are slightly rougher with a hint of bitterness. French and Californian are mild, lacking the piquancy of the others. Extra virgin olive oil is my standard for making vinaigrettes (other than for Asian dressings) as it complements almost everything.

Vegetable oils – Oils extracted from single species are labelled "pure"; others called "vegetable oil" are a mixture of different types. Most are low in cholesterol and comprised of monounsaturated or polyunsaturated fats. There are numerous types: corn, grape seed, rapeseed (canola), sunflower, soya and safflower oils being among the many. All share a mild, neutral taste that is useful for mayonnaise and other thick dressings.

accessories make the salad

GARLIC CROÛTONS

Not just for texture, garlic croûtons are perfect for soaking up the tart vinaigrette in any salad. Tomato and lettuce salads are particularly good with these.

200 g/7 oz sourdough bread, French stick or other quality bread, cut into 1 cm/½ inch cubes

4 tbsp extra virgin olive oil

2 garlic cloves, finely chopped

1 tsp salt

1 tsp freshly ground black pepper

Heat the oven to 200°C/400°F/Gas Mark 6.

Toss bread cubes with all the other ingredients on a large baking (cookie) sheet.

Bake for 8–10 minutes until light and golden. Avoid over-baking, as this will result in a rock hard rather than chewy centre.

Store in an airtight container for up to 2 days.

CRISPY SHALLOTS

Delicious on any South-east Asian salad with Thai Chilli Lime Dressing (see page 153), these are especially tasty with noodles.

600 ml/1 pint/2½ cups groundnut (peanut) or vegetable oil

12 shallots, very thinly sliced

125 g/4 oz/1 cup plain (all-purpose) flour

1 tsp salt

Heat the oil in small to medium, heavy saucepan.

Toss the shallots in the flour and shake off any excess. Test the temperature of the oil with a small piece of coated shallot; if it sizzles dramatically when added to the oil, the oil is ready.

Using a wire scoop, add the shallots to the hot oil, in batches if necessary. Fry for about 3 minutes until golden. Drain on kitchen paper (paper towels) and sprinkle with salt.

The shallots can be prepared 3 hours before using.

PITTA CROÛTONS

These are easy to make and ideal for added crunch in any salad.

6 pitta breads

4 tbsp extra virgin olive oil

1 tsp salt

1 tsp black pepper

Heat the oven to 200°/400°F/Gas Mark 6.

Cut the pittas into 1 cm/½ inch cubes. Separate the layers with your hands.

Place on a baking (cookie) sheet and toss with the olive oil, salt and pepper.

Bake for 8 minutes or until golden.

Store for up to 3 days in an airtight container.

OVEN-DRIED TOMATOES

Roasting tomatoes concentrates their sweetness and reduces the water inside them. These make a tremendous addition to beans, lentils or Caesar salad.

250 g/8 oz cherry or small plum tomatoes, halved

2 garlic cloves, finely chopped

2 tbsp extra virgin olive oil

1 tbsp balsamic vinegar

1 tsp salt

½ tsp freshly ground black pepper

Heat the oven to 160°C/325°F/Gas Mark 3.

Place the tomatoes, cut side up, on a large, non-stick baking (cookie) sheet.

Sprinkle the chopped garlic over them. Drizzle with the olive oil and balsamic vinegar and season with the salt and pepper.

Bake for 20–30 minutes until shrunken. Remove from baking (cookie) sheet.

The tomatoes can be prepared in the morning for serving in the evening.

PROSCIUTTO BITS

This easy topping complements lettuce, potato and legume salads.

6 slices prosciutto di Parma

Gently fry the prosciutto in a large, non-stick sauté pan for about 5 minutes until crispy. Remove from the pan and leave to cool.

Crumble the cooled prosciutto into small pieces.

If stored in airtight container, prosciutto bits can be prepared day before using.

ROASTED CAPERS

These are perfect for tossing on lettuce or potato salads.

4 tbsp capers, rinsed

1 tsp olive oil

Heat the oven to 200°C/400°F/Gas Mark 6.

Toss the capers with the oil in a small bowl and place on baking sheet. Roast for 6 minutes, then remove from the baking sheet.

The capers can be prepared in the morning to serve in the evening.

FRIED GINGER STICKS

Sprinkle these tasty batons over any Asian salad for a crispy assertive touch.

2.5 cm/1 inch piece of fresh root ginger, peeled

5 tbsp vegetable oil

Slice the ginger into very fine julienne.

Heat the oil in a medium sauté pan. Add the ginger and fry until golden and crispy. Drain on kitchen paper (paper towels).

Make them in the morning and store in airtight container for use in the evening.

CARAMELIZED NUTS

These nuts are so irresistible that they may never make it to the salad. Lettuce can be transformed by sprinkling with a few of them.

200 g/7 oz/1¾ cups nuts, such as pecans, hazelnuts, pistachios or walnuts

3 tbsp clear honey

½ tsp salt

2 tbsp caster (superfine) sugar

Heat the oven to 200°C/400°F/Gas Mark 6.

Toss the nuts with the honey, salt and sugar in a small bowl.

Place on a non-stick baking (cookie) sheet and spread out so that the nuts are not touching each other.

Bake for 3 minutes, remove from the baking sheet and place on non-stick baking parchment or greaseproof (wax) paper.

Caramelized nuts will keep well in jar with a tight-fitting lid for up to 2 weeks.

PARMESAN TUILES

These crisp little bites are elegant and easy to make, but it is essential to get the right non-stick baking parchment. They are great for whipping up an easy appetizer with a little rocket (arugula) and vinaigrette.

125 g/4 oz/1⅓ cups grated Parmesan cheese

Heat the oven to 200°C/400°F/Gas Mark 6 and line 2 baking (cookie) sheets with baking parchment.

Spoon the Parmesan on to the baking sheets into 12 small piles, spaced well apart. Flatten them into rounds.

Bake for 6–8 minutes until golden. Remove from oven and leave to stand for 1 minute to set. Using fish slice or thin spatula, remove the tuiles and place on wire rack to cool or drape over a rolling pin to cool and shape.

Parmesan tuiles can be prepared the day before if stored in an airtight container. You may want to re-crisp them in a hot oven for 1–2 minutes using same method as above.

index

This book is dedicated to my sister Teresa, the bravest person I know.

Author's acknowledgements

There are many people I want to thank for all of their support and assistance while producing this book:

My mother and father, for giving me passion for food and a great start to life. My husband Patrick, and sons Liam and Riley, for your love and patience while I tested recipes and worked long hours. Jean Hanson, my very special sister-in-law, for your invaluable feedback, editing and glorious sense of humor. Jennifer Thompson, my best friend, who always keeps me laughing and is my best supporter.

The team at Pavilion. Stuart Cooper, for believing in this book and making it happen. Emily Preece-Morrison, for calmly managing the details throughout the project. Sian Irvine, for taking such beautiful photography and making this book extraordinary. I had many happy chuckles during the long hours spent together in Hackney producing the photos. Andrew Barron, for your gorgeous design, good taste and dry wit. Lindsey Wilson, for your assistance at the photo-shoots and being such good company.

Victoria Blashford-Snell, for testing so many recipes, and being a great friend. A special acknowledgement to my friends, Penny Subbotin, Emma Leech, Emma Runyan, Nicki Elkins, Alison Purvis and Robin Ferrez for your honest feedback during our many enjoyable lunch "tastings". They were fun and extremely valuable.

Lindy Wifflin at *Ceramica Blue*, Aziz Hasham at *Voodoo Blue*, and *The White Company* for your kind loan of beautiful bowls, plates and linens.

Rosie Kindersley and Eric Truille, at *Books for Cooks*, for helping me develop the idea for this book, making critical introductions and being such supportive friends. Camilla Schneideman, at *Divertimenti*, for your boundless enthusiasm and hard work for my classes.

Publisher's acknowledgements

Many thanks to *China & Co.*, Linda Doeser and Caroline Hamilton.

This edition published in the U.S and Canada by Whitecap Books Ltd. For more information, contact Whitecap Books, 351 Lynn Avenue, North Vancouver, British Columbia, Canada, V7J 2C4

First published in Great Britain in 2004 by

PAVILION BOOKS LTD

The Chrysalis Building
Bramley Road
London W10 6SP

An imprint of Chrysalis Books Group plc

www.chrysalisbooks.co.uk

© Pavilion Books, 2004

Design/layout
© Pavilion Books, 2004

Text © Jennifer Joyce, 2004

Photographs © Sian Irvine, 2004

Commissioning Editor
Stuart Cooper

Project Editor
Emily Preece-Morrison

Designer and Art Director
Andrew Barron @ Thextension

Photographer
Sian Irvine

Food and Prop Styling
Jennifer Joyce

ISBN 1 55285 673 9

10 9 8 7 6 5 4 3 2 1

Printed by: Times Offset (M) Sdn. Bhd, Malaysia

Reproduction by: Mission Productions Ltd, Hong Kong